THE CORRESPONDENCE
THEORY OF TRUTH

PHILOSOPHY EDITOR
Professor S. Körner
jur.Dr., Ph.D., F.B.A.
Professor of Philosophy
University of Bristol and Yale University

The Correspondence Theory of Truth

D. J. O'CONNOR
*Professor of Philosophy
at the University of Exeter*

**HUTCHINSON
UNIVERSITY LIBRARY
LONDON**

HUTCHINSON & CO (Publishers) LTD
3 Fitzroy Square London W1

London Melbourne Sydney Auckland
Wellington Johannesburg Cape Town
and agencies throughout the world

First published 1975
© D. J. O'Connor 1975

Set in Monotype Times
Printed in Great Britain by The Anchor Press Ltd
and bound by Wm Brendon & Son Ltd
both of Tiptree, Essex

ISBN 0 09 123200 7

Contents

Preface

The title of this book may suggest more than its modest scope can offer, and the purpose of this preface is to say what I have and have not tried to do in writing it. In the first place, it is not an historical account of the Correspondence Theory. That would not be possible in a book of this size. (For anyone who needs a short account of the development of the theory, A. N. Prior's article in Paul Edwards' *Encyclopedia of Philosophy* could not be bettered.)

The earliest use of the term 'correspondence' in English to refer to 'verbal truth' is traced by the *Oxford English Dictionary* to the year 1809. This occurs not in the writings of a philosopher but in an article by the poet and critic S. T. Coleridge. About 100 years later, the Oxford Idealist philosopher, Harold Joachim, was writing of 'the correspondence theory of truth' in a book devoted to upholding a rival theory, though, as Prior says, the currency of the phrase in the present century is largely due to the writings of Bertrand Russell. But whatever the origins of the word 'correspondence' in this sense, the concept of truth as some kind of replica or map of reality is of ancient standing. '*Adaequatio intellectus et rei*', the phrase adopted by St Thomas Aquinas from Isaac Israeli, a medieval Jewish philosopher, expresses the same notion. Indeed, Joachim talks of a 'correspondence-notion' of truth in Aristotle and there is a famous quotation from the *Metaphysics* (1011b25) to bear him out: 'to say of what is that it is not, or of what is not that it is, is false, while to say of what is that it is or of what is not that it is not, is true'.

A large part of the interest of philosophers in the present century has been stimulated by the theories of Bertrand Russell and G. E. Moore. However, they have been so thoroughly dissected and criticized that I have not thought it useful to try to say more about them here. Nor have I examined the so-called 'picture theory' of Wittgenstein's *Tractatus*. When even experts in the interpretation of the *Tractatus* do not agree on the meaning to be attached to the term 'object', it would clearly be useless and impertinent for an outsider to add to the confusion. Further, I have avoided the difficult and important question of the truth value of empirical statements about the future. This is because its implications for the problems of free will and fatalism would be irrelevant in a book of this size.

What I have tried to do is, first, to examine the simplest statements of empirical fact and to try to see what we can mean when we say that such statements are true. In particular, I have considered whether any or all of beliefs, sentences, statements or propositions are properly said to be true or false. I have then tried to see what we mean by the term 'fact' and what possible relation between facts and beliefs (or their linguistic embodiments) could be meant by the term 'correspondence'.

In the second part of the book I have looked at a famous contemporary account of truth, Tarski's semantic theory, to see if it offers a satisfactory reconstruction of the essence of the traditional notion of correspondence. I then examine a recent well-known version of the correspondence theory, that of J. L. Austin and some criticisms of it by Professor P. F. Strawson. Finally I have tried to salvage whatever remnants of this view of truth seem to have survived criticism. This salvage operation does not result in a new version of the theory. But it does perhaps serve to re-direct our attention to those parts of philosophy that may hold the answers to the questions that the traditional theory has raised.

I am very grateful to the series editor, Professor Stephan Körner, for his patience and encouragement, to my colleagues Brian Carr, Avril Henry, Geoffrey Keene, Betty Powell and Colin Wright for help and criticism and to Mrs Peggy Martin and Mrs Genie Ridgeon for their expert secretarial skills.

D. J. O'CONNOR

Part I

1 | Introduction

The problems of philosophy arise from many sources—from scientific theories, from religious speculations and doctrines, from legal and political notions and also from concepts which are familiar to us all in everyday life. In particular, the problems of the theory of knowledge, though they are sharpened by the discoveries of physics, physiology and psychology, arise in the first place from perfectly familiar notions. We talk of seeing, hearing, remembering, believing and knowing, of truth and falsity and so on without any awkwardness or puzzlement. To say that I am now seeing trees and grass, that I am now remembering walking on an Irish beach a month ago, that I believe that the steady state theory of the universe is false are all fairly trivial and uninteresting statements, useful only as illustrating the point that I want now to make. That point is that these everyday concepts of seeing, memory, truth and belief are quite transparent and unproblematic when used in these ordinary contexts. But once we try to focus our attention on them and ask ourselves what exactly we mean by the words 'seeing', 'remembering', 'believe', 'true' and the like we meet quite unexpected difficulties. It is surprising and even paradoxical to find that concepts and their counterparts in language that we can handle effortlessly in ordinary discourse are not only very difficult to elucidate but are apt to lead us into a maze of inter-connected problems when we try to get our ideas clear about them.

The work of the philosopher is in some respects like that of the scientist. Each uses rational methods in dealing with his problems, each looks beneath surface appearance to explain the workings of what he is studying and each tries to link up his different areas of investigation into a consistent overall picture. It is true that the philosopher does not use the observational and experimental approach to the world which is the mark of natural science. His field of enquiry is conceptual rather than material. But his aim of a synoptic explanatory map of our conceptual world is very like what the scientist is looking for in his investigations into the workings of the physical world. In some ways, indeed, the natural scientist has the advantage in that the bits and pieces of the scientific jigsaw can be searched for one by one provided only that, when discovered, they fit together to make a comprehensible picture. An understanding of the nature of light, for example, was arrived at independently of an understanding of the nature of electricity before the genius of Maxwell brought the two fields of enquiry together into one theory. It is not so easy in philosophy to use the scientist's policy of 'divide and rule'. One problem leads very quickly to another so that if I ask, for example, exactly what I mean by saying that I *believe* a certain proposition *p*, I find very quickly that I have to ask the same question about the meanings of 'know', 'true', 'false' and many other words. All such concepts are linked together in a complex and widely ramifying network so that the satisfactory analysis of each seems to presuppose, quite impossibly, the analysis of all. In this unsatisfactory situation we have to compromise in the interest of arriving at some provisional solutions. These, we may hope, will offer a basis, however imperfect and insecure, for further more solidly based solutions to our problems.

These remarks are made by way of a preliminary warning about the limitations of this book. The topic that I shall be discussing is a particular theory about truth—the so-called correspondence theory. A 'theory' about truth is an attempt to give satisfactory answers to questions such as the following: what are the marks that distinguish a true statement from a false one? How can we establish that a particular statement is true or false? What is an acceptable definition of the word 'true'? Or, more simply, what is truth? Such questions do not look on the surface very difficult. But the attempt to answer them leads us very quickly into deep philosophical issues which have not so far met with any solutions that have been generally accepted.

Part of the difficulty with such questions is that they are very general. We can see at once the difference between asking:

(A) How can we establish that a particular statement is true or false?

and

(B) How can we establish that the statement 'There are orchids in Kew Gardens' is true or false?

We would all feel much happier about tackling (B) than (A) because it raises a particular concrete issue which our everyday experience has equipped us to deal with. Faced with question (A), the prudent answer seems to be: '*What* particular statement or what *kind* of statement are you talking about?' There is an indefinitely large number of possible questions and a large number of different *types* of question about which the issue of truth or falsity can be raised. Consider (B) in the general form (B'): How can we establish that the statement S is true or false? where S can be any one of the following statements:

1. There is at least one lion in the London Zoo
2. There are snakes in Ireland
3. Cigarette smoking causes lung cancer
4. The atomic weight of copper is 63·54
5. 1913 is a prime number
6. There is an infinite number of prime numbers
7. Abortion is wrong
8. God created the world
9. Every even number is the sum of two primes

This list could be made much longer but the examples given are sufficient to illustrate the point that the answer that we give to questions of the form (B') must depend on the nature of the statement occurring in the question. The methods by which we determine the truth value* of 1 are easy to state. We find out if there is at least one lion in the Zoo by going to look. More elaborate methods are needed to establish the truth values of 2, 3 and 4, though they are all similar to 1 and to each other in requiring sensory observation of some kind as a basis. 5 and 6 call for different methods; but the methods themselves, those of mathematics, are not in doubt. 7 and 8 are controversial in that there is no agreement about the ways in which statements of these two types can be confirmed or refuted or even, indeed, if they are genuine statements possessing truth values. 9 is an

---

*The term 'truth value' is a convenient accepted shorthand for the phrase 'truth or falsity'.

example of a mathematical statement whose truth or falsity has never been decided although mathematicians have worked on it for over 200 years.

Instances of this kind make it clear that we cannot profitably start upon the investigation of the nature of truth and its associated problems without first specifying what type of statement we are proposing to consider. Let us then agree to confine our attention to *empirical* statements. These are statements whose truth values can be determined, if they can be determined at all, by the evidence of the senses together with inferences made from such sensory evidence. Statements 1 to 4 above are instances of empirical statements. It should be emphasized, however, that it is very difficult to define the term 'empirical statements' exactly enough to know whether any given statement is empirical or not. It is a class which includes many different types. But the rather vague characterization given above will at least exclude from our field of interest statements of the types 5 to 9 above, together with many others. We need not concern ourselves with statements in mathematics, logic, moral philosophy, theology, aesthetics, politics and so on except in so far as they can plausibly be construed as empirical. (Contrast, for example, two statements which may arise in a political context: 'Democracy is the most stable form of government', 'Democracy is the best form of government'. The first is an empirical statement supported, in so far as it can be supported, by historical evidence. The second is not.)

This somewhat crude and naive distinction will enable us to select for investigation a more manageable field of enquiry than would be the case if we were prepared to envisage a theory of truth which would claim to account for all ascriptions of truth values to statements. The difficulties even of this restricted field are, as we shall see, quite formidable enough.

2 | Preconditions for a theory of truth

In a famous version of the correspondence theory of truth,[1] published over sixty years ago, Bertrand Russell laid down three conditions which must be satisfied by any attempt to answer the question: what do we *mean* by truth and falsehood? (1) The account that we give of truth must allow for the possibility of falsehood and error. The only reason for stating this seemingly obvious condition is that philosophers have offered accounts of truth in the past which did not fulfil this condition. (2) Truth and falsity must be properties of beliefs and statements. A world without consciousness and so without symbols in which to register and convey the contents of consciousness would have no place for truth. (3) Lastly, though truth and falsehood are notions attributable only to beliefs and statements, they are not attributable in virtue of any intrinsic property of the belief itself—its clarity, for example, or the certainty with which it is held. A belief must be true in virtue of something external to the belief itself but to which the belief is in some way related. We usually say that beliefs are true or false because of their relation to *facts*. We shall be asking later exactly what this means; but for the present we need only note it as a prerequisite of the enquiry. These conditions conform fairly well to our rather vague intuitive notions of truth and falsity. And we should perhaps add a fourth condition: (4) truth and falsity are properties that belong *once and for all* to belief, statement or whatever else we may agree to select as our truth-bearers. It is difficult to put any sense on the supposition that a statement or belief once true or false could afterwards change its truth values. (This is not to say, of course, that we cannot change our cognitive attitudes to a given statement so that it is accepted as true at one time and not at another.)

It might indeed be asked whether we are not improperly limiting

[1] Superior figures refer to Notes and references, pp. 137-9.

the field of our enquiry by stating preconditions for the answer in this way. Are we not perhaps begging the question that we are considering by setting limits in advance to the answers that we shall find acceptable? This is a difficulty with which any philosophical enquiry is faced, and, to some extent, any scientific enquiry as well. All questions, however they are posed, must set the framework for their answers. This is so whether the question is of the Yes/No type or of what the linguists call the *Wh*-type which calls for an answer in terms of a description. In the case of Yes/No questions, the issue is clear. If I phone the station to ask, 'Is the 10.30 from London on time?' the form of my question allows only two acceptable answers (provided, of course, that my informant does not reply with 'Don't know' which is not an answer to the question). Questions of the *Wh*-type specify implicitly a wider range of possible answers. But that there is such an implicitly assumed range is clear from the fact that we reject some answers as absurd or irrelevant. (For example, 'Where is the dog?' may plausibly be answered with 'In the garden' or 'On the sofa' but not with 'On the dome of St Paul's' or 'At the court of Queen Anne'.)

In general, we can say that it is the mark of a precisely phrased question that it has a clear range of acceptable answers. Most ordinary everyday questions are of this convenient type. But some scientific questions and most of those that arise in philosophy are not. Some of the peculiar puzzlement that such questions generate arises from the fact that it is difficult to say what kind of an answer we expect. Part of the remedy for this unsatisfactory state of affairs is to take care to make the question we are asking as precise as possible. That is to say, we have to make clear to ourselves, at least, what kind of an answer we would find acceptable. And we have to do this in the knowledge that it is a dangerous procedure. It is dangerous because by delimiting the range of possible answers to our question to accommodate our ignorance or our prejudice we may thereby exclude the right answer. Errors of this kind are familiar in the history of science.

It is considerations of this sort that are the main justification for the constraints that we have already placed on the answers to our question: what is truth? For example, we first limited the range of the question to empirical statements and then further specified that any acceptable answer to the question must conform to four conditions. We do have, however, some further justification for restricting the range of the enquiry in this way.

Our justification is that, as we noted earlier, 'true' and 'truth' are ordinary English words whose meanings are familiar. They are vague words in that their exact range of application is indeterminate. But their central core of meaning is well enough understood to justify us in anticipating the general outlines of the answers that we are looking for. When we read in the *Oxford English Dictionary* that an important meaning of 'truth' is 'conformity with fact; agreement with reality', we recognize in this accepted social usage a very rough blue-print for our investigation. The so-called correspondence theory of truth is simply an attempt to spell out in consistent detail the implications of the accepted dictionary definition.

It must be conceded, however, that the use of the word 'theory' in the phrase 'correspondence theory of truth' is misleading. The standard uses of the term 'theory' occur in the context of the natural sciences where the term means roughly 'a logically connected set of hypotheses'. But we must have an idea of what we mean by 'true' and 'false' before we can even begin to formulate a hypothesis. For a hypothesis is something to be tested and confirmed or falsified. And we would not know what it meant to confirm or falsify a hypothesis if we did not already have some notion of what we meant by 'true' and 'false'. However, it is an important function of a theory to be a vehicle of *explanation*. And it is certainly an essential task of a philosophical account of truth to explain the concept adequately, to remove as far as is possible the penumbra of vagueness that surrounds its everyday occurrences, to elucidate its detail and to trace its linkages with related concepts. In so far as the correspondence theory (or any other theory) of truth attempts to do this, it may, by a loose analogy, be called a theory.

The correspondence theory of truth may be regarded as a systematic development of the commonsense account of truth embodied in such dictionary definitions for 'truth' as 'conformity with fact' and the like. Taken at their face value, such definitions seem to be straightforward and uncontroversial. If, however, it is found that they cannot be developed systematically without disclosing inconsistencies and contradictions, this will be evidence that our commonsense ideas on the subject of truth and its allied notions, for all their surface acceptability, are covertly incoherent and need reformulation in the interests of intellectual hygiene.

3 | Truth and verification

Most philosophical accounts of truth start with a warning against confusing two different but closely allied questions: (a) What is truth? (b) How do we find out what beliefs are true? (a) is a question about the nature of truth; (b) is a question about the nature of verification. The first is a theoretical question; the second is more practical. Most people can go through their lives without raising the philosophical issues of (a); but the demands of everyday living require that we all have some answer, however imperfect, to (b). Bertrand Russell claimed, indeed, that the question of verification which he put in the form 'How are we to know, in a given case, that our belief is not erroneous?' is 'a question of the very greatest difficulty, to which no completely satisfactory answer is possible'. And he added that the question: what do we *mean* by truth and falsehood? was less difficult. It is worthwhile to get clear at the start of our discussion what the relations between these two questions are.

To the extent that no satisfactory *general* answer to the question: how do we verify our beliefs? is possible, it must be admitted that Russell is right. But this question is an impossibly difficult one only because it is too general. It is similar in this respect to questions like 'How do doctors cure diseases?' or even 'How do you entertain your friends?' To such over-general questions, one can only reply with the vacuous formula: 'Some in one way, some in another.' Some of our beliefs are verified by personal observation, some by inference from known facts, some by checking authorities and so on. There can be no general formula.

However, it is clear that these two questions are not independent. The answer that we give to one will affect the answer that we give to the other. To verify a given belief means to establish it as true. It is therefore a necessary condition for the verification of a belief that we should be able to give some rough description of the conditions under which the belief will be accepted as true. Conversely, it is hard to understand how a belief can be reckoned to be true if we have no idea at all of how it could be verified. We shall have occasion later to look more closely at these points. But if we admit, as it seems that we must, that questions about the nature of truth and about verification are connected in this way, are we not faced with a difficulty at the outset of our enquiry into the nature of empirical truth?

I have conceded that the question: how do we know that a given belief is true? does not admit of any general answer; but if it is the case that each individual belief or proposition which is a candidate for being assigned a truth value must be considered on its own logical merits and that its truth must be tested by the methods appropriate to a belief or proposition of this kind, what becomes of the claim that we can give a general definition or analysis of the concept of truth? If there is little in common between methods of verification, how can there be a unitary concept of truth? This difficulty must be borne in mind in the light of later discussion. But two points may be made at once. (1) That there are many methods of verification does not entail that there are many concepts of truth. The same thing may sometimes be discovered by many different methods. (2) It is not the case that each individual belief or proposition has a unique method of verification peculiar to itself. It is rather that each logically distinct type of empirical proposition has a mode of testing appropriate to its nature. Some statements indeed may reasonably be held to have a truth value even though we do not know or cannot apply a procedure of testing for that value. But it must be conceded that the fact that logically distinct types of statement are held to be distinct partly in virtue of their distinct logical structures does raise serious problems for the notion of correspondence as a basis for the truth-relation. All these points will be looked at in more detail as the argument develops.

4 | Two uses of 'true' and 'truth'

Phrases like 'The witness was speaking the truth' have two distinct meanings. They can mean that what was being said was in conformity with fact. Or they can—and perhaps more commonly—mean that what was said was in conformity with what the speaker *believed* to be the facts. To say 'John always tells the truth' is not to claim that he is infallible but merely that he never says what he believes not to be the case. Thus 'true' predicated of an utterance can mean either (a) that the utterance accurately expresses the belief which it communicates or (b) that *in addition to* (a), the belief itself is in conformity with the facts. Thus 'true' can relate to a conformity, correspondence or agreement between belief and its verbal expression or between a belief and the facts to which it relates. Thus a verbal expression capable of being assigned a truth value can fail in two ways to be a genuine *truth-bearer*; either because due to the speaker's intention or otherwise it fails to express his belief; or because his belief is itself mistaken.

This point is important for two reasons. First, it seems to support the view that *beliefs* are the primary or basic vehicles of truth or falsity. And, in consequence, verbal or other symbolic expressions of belief are true or false only in a derivative sense. But, secondly, it seems to suggest that there are two different occurrences of the relation of conformity or correspondence involved in every case of ostensible statement. First, our beliefs must claim a correspondence with facts. And then the verbal expression of the belief must correspond to the belief itself. We are not in a position at this stage to say whether or not these different occurrences of the correspondence relation are instances of the same relation or not. Perhaps they are two different kinds of correspondence or conformity. But if we recognize that there are these different occurrences of some kind of relation of corre-spondence, we shall not be deceived into thinking that the problem is simpler than it really is.

So far, what I have said has consisted merely of rather informal and loosely phrased preliminaries to the discussion. Let us now try to state the problem in more detail but still at the level of 'enlightened commonsense'.

The word 'true' is an English adjective and it is an ordinary function of adjectives in English that they stand for *properties* or *qualities*. This does not tell us much for properties may be of very different kinds; and the apparent workings of even familiar language may be a poor guide to its real workings. Nevertheless, a preliminary investigation of the grammar of a word can act as a sort of range finder for closer and more detailed examination of its meaning. And it is obviously part of our task in investigat-ing the correspondence theory of truth to get as clear as possible about the meaning of the word 'true'.

One obvious way of raising the question: *what kind of* a property is Q? is to ask: what kind of things does Q qualify? But this aid is not available to us here because one of the principal difficulties that we meet in discussing truth is to determine exactly what range of entities can properly be called 'true'. (We have already talked informally of beliefs, propositions and statements being true. But this informal usage ignores one of the main questions that we have to face. These words 'belief', 'proposition' and 'statement' are not self-evidently synonyms.) What kinds of properties are there? Two principles of division can be used: first, how do we come to know that something has the property? Secondly, how many things does one occurrence of the property qualify?

As regards the first of these, some properties are known immediately in experience. That something is red, hot or sweet can be established in ordinary circumstances by sensory tests, by looking, tasting and so on. But clearly we do not establish that a belief or a statement is true in such ways. Truth is not a property that beliefs and statements wear on their sleeves, so to speak. There are, of course, some kinds of statement that are commonly said to be 'self-evidently' or 'intuitively' true. That two plus three equals five or that seven is a prime number might perhaps qualify to be known as true in the direct way that sugar is known to be sweet. Substantial philosophical doubts can be raised about this concept of self-evidence but we do not have to consider the point here. For it is only in respect of *non-empirical* propositions that the claim can plausibly be made that their truth values can be immediately known. And we have agreed to confine our attention to empirical propositions. There is another class of properties which are evinced only in special circumstances and which are not known to be present in their absence. For example, that something is fragile, poisonous, soluble or magnetic cannot be descried by simple sensory observation. Such adjectives relate to what are called dispositional properties, qualities which are latent in most circumstances but which are made manifest in special conditions. X is fragile if and only if it breaks when dropped; Y is poisonous if and only if it causes illness or death when eaten; and so on. Again it is clear that truth is not a property of this sort. (For example, we could say, without committing ourselves to a vicious circle, that P is true if and only if it is verified or verifiable. For the concept of truth is basic to the concept of verification.) A third and very important class of properties are those which can be known only as a result of inference. For example, that X is made of silver, that Y is monatomic, that Z contains sulphur are instances of properties that are knowable only as the outcome of evaluating evidence in a rational way. There is a wide range of adjectives and descriptive phrases (adjectivals, as they are sometimes called) that fall into this category. Indeed, it might be argued that dispositional properties, considered above, are just a special class of this third kind of property.

Can we say then that truth is such a property? For it is clear that if I claim that a given empirical statement is true, I must be prepared, if my claim is not merely frivolous, to offer evidence on the basis of which I assert its truth. The answer to this question is Yes; but the Yes must be carefully qualified if it is not to be misleading. If I confirm my belief that my pen is in the top drawer of my desk by opening the drawer and looking or if I confirm my belief that compound A contains sulphur by performing the appropriate chemical test, I am so to speak doing two things at once. I confirm that something has a certain property and, at the same time, I confirm that the proposition that the thing in question has that property is true. Or it would be less misleading to say that I confirm that the proposition is true by confirming that the thing has the property in question. The only way that we can confirm that a given proposition has the property of being true is by confirming that some feature of the world has some *other* property. Thus truth may well be a property whose existence in a given case we establish by inference. But it is a derivative or second-order property.

At this point a sceptic might suggest that it is not so much derivative as vacuous. Suppose that P is the proposition 'There are six protons in the carbon atom'. What is then required for P to be true further than that there are in fact six protons in a carbon atom? And if nothing further is required how does asserting that P is true differ from asserting that P? This again is a question that must be faced later in the discussion. For the present, we may note that there does appear to be something more required for the truth of P, namely, that the words used in stating P should have the meanings that they have in English and that the syntax of English is such that those words, in that order, convey the information content of P. For truth is a property of beliefs and their expressions.

The second principle of division mentioned above was: how many things does one occurrence of a property qualify? For example, if a given tomato is red, one occurrence of the property *red* qualifies only one thing, namely, the tomato in question. But many properties, the so-called relational properties, need to qualify two or more individuals at the same time in order to occur at all. Contrast, for instance:

10. This line is blue
11. This line is parallel

The term 'blue' is a one-place predicate in the terminology of modern logic. But 'parallel' is a two-place predicate and 11 is elliptical for

12. This line is parallel to some other line

And it is clear that 'true' is much more analogous to 'parallel' than it is to one-place predicates like 'red' or 'fragile' or 'monatomic'. So much indeed is obvious simply from our acceptance of the third of Russell's preconditions for a theory of truth. Although 'true' is a property of beliefs or their symbolic formulations, a belief (or its expression) must be true in virtue of something external to the belief itself but to which the belief is *in some way* related. Truth then is a relational property and a theory of truth must spell out the nature of the relation.

So far then, I have suggested that 'true' is a second-order relational property of beliefs and their symbolic expressions which is discovered by inference. This rough preliminary range-finding suggests two further questions: (1) What kind of inference is required? (2) What kind of a relation is truth?

The first question has already been raised in a slightly different guise as: how do we verify our beliefs? For to find out that P is true is to verify it. And we saw that there could be no general answer to such a question. How we determine the truth of a particular proposition will depend upon the logical character of the proposition. And the fact that propositions can differ widely in their logical characters will raise problems when we are trying to decide precisely what could be meant by saying that truth consists in the correspondence of beliefs or propositions with facts. Nor is the second question any easier at this stage of the enquiry. Logicians classify relations in terms of the presence or absence of certain standard properties, in particular, reflexivity, symmetry and transitivity.* But we do not know enough about this particular relation to be able to say with any assurance how it is to be classified in these terms. 'True of' is presumably an irreflexive and asymmetrical relation. For if we have a belief B and a fact F, we can say (a) B is not true of itself and (b) if B is

*Logicians divide relations according to the number of individuals involved in the relation. *Dyadic* or *binary* relations which connect two individuals ('larger than' or 'loves' for example), have the following important properties. A relation is *transitive* if when, if A has r to B and B has r to C, then A has r to C. For example, 'larger than' or 'equal to' are transitive. A relation is *symmetrical* if, when A has r to B, then B has r to A. For example, 'equal to' or 'sibling of' are symmetrical. A relation is *reflexive* if it is such that it holds between any individual and itself. For example, 'equal to' and 'identical with' are reflexive relations. *Intransitive, asymmetrical* and *irreflexive* are properties of relations for which the properties illustrated above *cannot* hold. For example, 'father of' is an asymmetrical, intransitive and irreflexive relation, since if A is the father of B, B cannot be the father of A; if A is father of B and B of C, then A cannot be father of C; and no one can be his own father. Relations may also be non-symmetrical, non-transitive or non-reflexive if the given properties may or may not hold. For example, 'teaches' or 'loves' are non-symmetrical and non-transitive relations. 'Loves' is a non-reflexive relation since one may or may not love oneself.

true of F, then F is not true of B. But is it transitive? On the one hand we might argue like this: given a proposition P, a belief B and a fact F, if P is true of B and B is true of F then P is true of F. But this begs a very important question: is the sense of 'true' in which an expression is said to be true if it correctly reflects my belief the same as the sense of 'true' in which my belief may be said to be true to the facts? We have seen already that to say 'The witness was speaking the truth' may mean either 'He was speaking the truth *as he saw it*' or 'He was speaking the truth *as it actually was*'. It is clear that at this stage of the argument, we do not know enough about the relation 'true of' to be able to answer such questions with confidence.

5 | Beliefs and their expression

I said earlier that one way of raising the question: what kind of a property is Q? is to ask: what kind of things does Q qualify? The answer to this question was deferred because it raises a very large and complex issue. The question: what is a truth-bearer? is central to any enquiry about the nature of truth and it must now be faced. So far, we have talked loosely and indifferently of beliefs and their expression (as propositions or statements) being true or false. It was indeed suggested that it is beliefs that are the primary or basic truth-bearers and that the symbolic expressions of belief are true or false in a secondary or derivative sense. This point must be elaborated a little as it has important consequences.

Consider the following case. A, who knows little of natural history, sees a bird in the garden which he thinks will interest his wife, who is a keen bird-watcher. He calls to her, 'There is a bull-finch on the bird table.' The bird is, in fact, a chaffinch, although A believes it to be a bullfinch. In this case, S, the statement, is a true expression of A's belief although the belief is false. Thus we have, S is true of B and B is false of F; giving S is false of F.

Now contrast this with a second case. A sees a bullfinch on the bird table but takes it to be a chaffinch. Wishing to tease his wife he calls out, 'There is a bullfinch on the bird table.' In this case, S is false of B and B is false of F. But S is nevertheless true of F, since S is the statement that there is a bullfinch on the bird table and F is the fact that there is a bullfinch there. Thus in the first case, we have S true of B and B false of F, giving S false of F. And in the second, the two relations of falsity between S and B and B and F respectively yield S true of F.

The second case must not be taken to suggest that for all cases of S, B and F, S will be true of F if S is false of B and B false of F. For it is easy to imagine cases where a false belief and a false statement of the belief together yield a statement which is false of the facts. (Suppose there is a bullfinch on the table which A believes to be a chaffinch. But he falsely reports his belief by saying that there is a hoopoe on the table.) Such cases lead us to suppose that either 'true' stands for a non-transitive relation or, more plausibly, that there are two entirely different senses of 'true' at issue here. If this is so, we have to decide what these senses are and how they are related to one another.

Let us provisionally distinguish these two senses as *truth of expression* and *truth of cognition* respectively. Then truth of expression will be a relation holding between a belief and its adequate formulation in a language or other symbolic system. And truth of cognition will be a relation holding between a belief and the fact which the belief represents. The first type of truth will depend upon the meaning rules of the language in question; the second will depend upon the way in which facts can be represented in beliefs. But this distinction has the disadvantage of making cognitive truth the basic concept and so *beliefs* rather than propositions, statements, sentences or utterances the basic truth-bearers. But if we still wish to retain a concept of truth which relates beliefs *and their expressions* with objective states of affairs, we must be prepared to recognize that truth is a two-layered concept, so to speak. To say that some symbolic formulation of a belief is true is to say *both* that the formulation is adequate to the belief in terms of the rules of the language *and also* that the belief is true. Some philosophers, indeed, have tried to eliminate the notion of belief from their analysis of truth altogether and talk simply of truth as a relation between linguistic expressions and facts. Each of these approaches has its own difficulties and disadvantages, as we shall see.

One argument may usefully be introduced at this stage, in favour of retaining the two-layered concept of truth as expressive and as cognitive. If we consider the four possible ways in which we can combine true and false beliefs with true and false affirmations, respectively, we get the following:

(i) A believes (truly) that P and says, 'P'.
(ii) A believes (truly) that P and says, 'not-P'.
(iii) A believes (falsely) that P and says, 'P'.
(iv) A believes (falsely) that P and says, 'not-P'.

Cases (i), (ii) and (iii) put constraints on the truth of the statement 'P' relative to the objective facts referred to. In case (i), the statement must be true and in cases (ii) and (iii) it must necessarily be false. Only in case (iv) (as we saw earlier in the matter of the bullfinch, chaffinch and hoopoe) is the outcome indeterminate. In other words, if we accept the expressive–cognitive distinction, we may conclude that the presence of *either* cognitive truth *or* expressive truth guarantees that the composite truth relation of proposition to fact is clearly determined. In the absence of both expressive and cognitive truth, the truth value of the proposition is undecided and can be either true or false depending on the individual facts of the case.

We must now look more closely at the candidates for the status of truth-bearer. In the course of the philosophical controversy about truth the following have been suggested: beliefs, judgements, propositions, statements, sentences, utterances. These, at least, are the principal applicants for the status. Beliefs seem to have a certain priority here as it is prima facie a necessary condition of a statement or other symbolic vehicle of a belief having a truth value that the belief itself should have one. At the same time, it seems that a belief may be true or false even if it has not been expressed in language. At least we shall be in a better position to understand what we mean by 'proposition', 'statement' and the rest when we have made clearer what we understand by 'belief'.

Let us begin with our unsophisticated commonsense notion of belief. One of the principal definitions offered in the *Concise Oxford Dictionary* is 'acceptance as true of any statement, fact, etc.' This is uncontroversial but unhelpful, as it embodies the word 'true' as part of the definition. And it is the exact anatomy of the concept of truth that we are at present seeking. Let us try to do two things with this commonsense concept: first, let us put it under the microscope, so to speak, so that it can be looked at in closer detail. Secondly, let us try to trace some of its connections with allied concepts so that we can make the meaning that we attach to the term more precise by examining its conceptual context.

Like most terms relating to mental processes and events, 'belief' has a double meaning. It can refer to a mental state or to the object to which the state is directed. If we talk of a belief being faint or vivid, confident or vacillating, we are referring to the act or process of believing and not to the content of the belief. But if we talk of a belief as being well evidenced or irrational or, especially, true or false, we are referring not to any mental act, process or state but to the *content* or *object* of the belief. If I am a twentieth-century astronomer, I will believe strongly and confidently that the sun is the centre of our planetary system. And the object of this belief—that the sun is the centre of our planetary system—is well supported by evidence and, so far as we are able to say, true. A similar act–content distinction can be made in respect of other mental acts or states—perception, sensation, memory, fear, hope, wishes and the rest. There is no agreed term for the object of our beliefs, memories, perceivings, hopes and so on which we introduce by that-clauses: A believes that . . .; I hope that . . .; John remembers that. . . . The term 'proposition' which we have used informally before often serves this purpose; I shall use it here and look more closely at its meaning later.

A second important distinction to be made in respect of 'belief' is that we may speak of belief in two further senses, belief as a disposition or semi-permanent state of the organism and belief as a mental occurrence. The astronomer mentioned above believes that the sun is the centre of our planetary system but he very rarely adverts consciously to the proposition in question. His belief amounts to little more than a disposition to affirm the proposition if occasion requires it (if, for example, he is debating with a flat-earther). We do not say that a man's beliefs cease to exist when they are not being contemplated. On the contrary, they exist in the same way as the brittleness of glass still exists when the glass is not being subjected to shock or the solubility of sugar still exists when it is not immersed in water. However, though most of our beliefs for most of the time are in this state of suspended animation, there is another and very important sense of the word 'belief'. The basic evidence that we have for any disposition is that it eventuates in action from time to time. Occurrent cases of believing are the assents or rejections that we make in respect of propositions. And these occurrent instances of believing must, it is obvious, be prior to and basic to the disposition. In order to have a disposition to affirm that the sun is the centre of the planetary system, the astronomer must at some prior time have learned and assented to the proposition. For our dispositions to believe are not innate.

If we accept this distinction, as it seems that we must, there is another to be recognized. What kind of event is to count as an occurrence of a given belief? We have talked so far naively in terms of *mental* events. But many philosophers have denied that there are any such events and have claimed instead that anything which can be described or explained by assuming their existence can be accounted for equally well by talking of observable *behaviour*. It is certainly the case that we infer the existence of beliefs in other people simply on the evidence of their behaviour, including their use of language. This must be so simply because we can have no direct awareness of the contents of the consciousness of another person. Even in our own case, we often catch ourselves evincing by some piece of spontaneous and unplanned behaviour a belief in some proposition to which we had not consciously adverted. Suppose, for example, that I bend to pick up what I suppose to be a heavy weight but is, in fact, a piece of wood painted to resemble such a weight. I will automatically have made all the muscular adjustments appropriate to lifting, say 60 lb. My surprise at the outcome tells me that I had taken for granted, without consciously assenting to, the proposition, 'This is a heavy weight.'

It is clear then that some occurrent beliefs are manifested as bits of behaviour. We need not pursue the question whether such a behavioural account of all beliefs is possible. I do not think that it is for reasons that I have explained elsewhere.[2] But certainly some beliefs can be evinced in this way. And, if we extend the meaning of the term 'behaviour' to include the use of language, linguistic behaviour, a great deal of the expression of belief seems to be behavioural. And since any sincere expression of a belief is an assent to the proposition that the belief embodies, a great deal of occurrent beliefs are symbolized in bits of behaviour. But because these bits of behaviour—phrases, sentences, gestures and so on—are *symbols*, a complete account of the expression of the belief calls for an account, difficult to give in behavioural terms, of the intentions of the speaker and the understanding of his audience. Thus although we can give a plausible description of a good deal of belief in terms of behaviour, there is a patent gulf between pieces of behaviour considered merely as physical events and the same behaviour illuminated, so to speak, by intentions and understanding. And it is such concepts as these which seem to introduce an ineradicably private and non-physical element into the concept of occurrent believing.

How are the distinctions made so far relevant to the notion of belief as a truth-bearer? Clearly we are concerned with the *content* and not the *act* of believing and with beliefs as concrete *occurrences* and not as mere *dispositions*. And the occurrences which express the content of beliefs are commonly, though not always, symbolically coded, usually in some natural language. Philosophers are apt to take as their standard cases of belief well-evidenced empirical propositions expressed in fairly precise language. These are the evolutionary peak, so to speak, of our beliefs. But we must remember that the inchoate tendencies to action of animals and small children often embody beliefs. The dog may evince without language his belief that he has a bone buried in the corner of the garden. That belief will be true or false. But what, in such cases, is the belief to which we attribute a truth value? The difficulty of answering that question makes us prefer to treat the philosopher's more sophisticated standard case. But we must surely recognize the artificiality of an approach to the question: how is a belief a truth-bearer? via the sentences in which the beliefs are expressed. The vast majority of our beliefs neither merit nor require formulation in language. As we saw above in the case of the weight lifter's mistake, one of the commonest ways in which we are brought to realize that we have held a particular belief is our surprise when experience fails to bear it out. We attribute, with good reason, beliefs to animals and infants and other creatures without linguistic skills.

Nevertheless, there are many important beliefs which could not be entertained without linguistic or other symbolic expression. It will therefore be a useful preliminary to talking about the ways in which sentences, statements, propositions and the like can be true or false, to review the main consequences of putting beliefs into linguistic form.

(a) We can make a belief more precise and detailed by expressing it in language. And by carefully qualifying and elaborating the statement that expresses the belief we can increase without limit the exactness of the expression and so the detailed content of the belief. (This is just a special case of the surprising but indubitable fact that the process of expressing our thoughts in words enables us to know more exactly just what we are thinking.)

(b) A belief unformulated in words tends to be fluctuating and unstable in content as well as imprecise. By expressing it in a statement we precipitate the content, to use a chemical metaphor, and keep it unchanged for future reference.

(c) Many philosophers have explained belief in terms of a mental activity of contemplating or entertaining a proposition plus some further mental attitude of assent or doubt or rejection.[3] It is difficult to make sense of such a notion unless we are talking of believing statements expressed in language. It is obvious that we all believe many propositions long before we are capable of the fairly advanced feat of simply considering a proposition without adopting any attitude towards it. It follows that the project of elucidating the notion of believing P via the notion of entertaining P makes no sense below the fairly sophisticated level of opinions expressed in language. It is only when beliefs are given some symbolic expression that they acquire the precision and stability that enables us to entertain them.

Our conclusion so far is that if it is beliefs that are to be our truth-bearers, it must be beliefs as contents and beliefs as occurrent rather than dispositional. (It is not that dispositional beliefs are not true or false; but they can be said to be so only derivatively. They take their truth values from their concrete occurrences.) We have agreed further that though many of our beliefs are expressed in a language or other symbolic medium, such as the notation of mathematics, by no means all of them are so expressed. This raises the difficult question: is the sense in which an unexpressed belief is true the same as the sense in which a precise linguistic expression of the belief is true? It is a question which we cannot answer at this stage of the enquiry. But we must return to it when we have looked first at the ways in which beliefs take expression and then at the ways in which truth-bearers are related to facts.

As an appendix to this discussion of belief, we may look briefly at the term 'judgement'. This has been used, chiefly by philosophers of the idealist tradition, as the principal subject of the predicates 'true' and 'false'. But it raises no problems for us that are not already raised by belief. 'Judgement' is indeed a near synonym of 'belief' in the occurrent sense of the term. The difference between the two seems to be that 'judgement' conveys the notion of a deliberate and rationally supported assent. But this makes little difference to its status as a possible truth-bearer. Like beliefs, judgements can be unformulated or precisely stated. Even a carefully calculated rational decision may be embodied in a judgement unformulated in any symbolic medium. For example, at a certain stage in a game of chess, I may decide that bishop to king's knight five is the best move open to me. But I can make the decision and the move without saying anything publicly or even to myself.

6 | Linguistic truth-bearers

We must turn now to the distinctively linguistic forms in which beliefs and judgements may present themselves. We have already noticed that beliefs can carry truth values in the absence of linguistic expression and that a given formulation in language may express a belief adequately or may fail to do so. This seems to suggest that the truth of a judgement expressed in language is the outcome of a double relation—of the expression to the belief and of the belief to the facts of the case. Let us now ask what exactly are we supposing to be the expression of a given belief? Is it the sentence, the statement or the proposition? Do these terms mark useful or important distinctions or are they near synonyms? We may conveniently begin with the sentence. It seems at least to be a more reassuringly familiar notion than statement or proposition which are terms of art and consequently more difficult to explicate.

Any educated person can form and recognize sentences in his own native language. But this does not mean that we can say exactly what the term means. In any case, if we are looking for truth-bearers, it is clear that not all sentences can perform this task. For some sentences are questions and some are commands. Those sentences which are capable of being true or false, if any are, are indicative sentences which purport to describe states of affairs in the world. For example, I am now looking at the surface of the table before me and see a piece of green stone lying there. I write the sentence, 'There is a piece of green stone on the table.' It seems as clear as anything can be that the sentence I have just written is true. Indicative sentences of the type with which we are concerned describe situations and they may describe them correctly or otherwise. And if they describe them correctly, surely they should be called 'true'.

Yet however obvious this may seem, the question: can sentences be true or false? has occasioned sharp disagreement among philosophers. A famous version of the correspondence theory of truth, the so-called Semantic Theory, which we shall be considering in a later chapter, requires that sentences are truth-bearers. And Professor Price, writing from quite a different viewpoint in his recent Gifford Lectures,[4] suggests that to understand a sentence is to know 'what it would be like for the sentence to be true'. But other contemporary philosophers have denied that sentences can have truth values. Professor David Hamlyn, in his book *The Theory of Knowledge*, says 'it is clear that truth cannot be a property of sentences'.[5] Hamlyn's main reason for this conclusion is that a sentence is not 'a candidate for truth' until it is used to make a statement. I may, for example, use the sentence that I mentioned above:

13. There is a piece of green stone on the table

not in order to make an affirmation about an observable state of affairs but simply as a grammatical example. Suppose that I am teaching English to a Frenchman. I might use the sentence to show how to translate the French sentence, '*Il y a un morceau de pierre verte sur la table.*' And the sentence could not be then said to be true or false since it was being used as a grammatical example and not to make a statement.

This raises an important question. We may know what we mean by a sentence in the sense that we can all use our native speakers' intuition to form sentences and to recognize them. This is so even if we find that dictionary definitions are unsatisfactory and that linguists argue over the way the term is to be defined. But what do we mean by 'the same sentence' or 'one sentence'? Are the two occurrences of the sentence about the green stone above the same sentence or different sentences? This is clearly not a trivial question of terminology since I used the first occurrence of the phrase to describe a state of affairs and the second simply as a grammatical example divorced from any context or function of description. The first occurrence might be said to be true and the second to have no truth value. Suppose now that I utter the same sequence of words to describe another table now in front of me. There is no piece of stone there and the sentence could be said, in consequence, to be false. We now have three occurrences of the same sentence, of which the first is true, the second neither true nor false and the third false.

But if one and the same sentence can take sometimes different truth values and sometimes no truth value at all, it is clearly useless to look to sentences as our truth-bearers. We can now see the force of Hamlyn's point that sentences are not candidates for truth (or for falsity either) unless they are used to make *statements*. And there are several ways in which sentences can be used other than to make statements. To use them as grammatical examples is only one such use. If then we are to continue to talk about sentences usefully in this context, we have to introduce some necessary distinctions. If we speak of 'the same sentence' occurring in two places (as with our example about the green stone) we can speak of the same type-sentence or the same sentence-design occurring in two sentence-tokens or sentence-events or in two inscriptions or utterances. A type-sentence or sentence-design is just a string of words conforming to the grammatical rules of a natural language. A sentence-token or event* (or utterance or inscription) is a particular occurrence of that language pattern which can be put to varied *uses*. One (but only one) of these uses may be, in the case of indicative sentences, to make a statement. And it is the statement that has the truth value. If we are to call sentences true or false, we have to recognize that they are called so only in a secondary sense which they take from their statement-making function. They cannot exert their truth-carrying authority in their own right.

The outcome of this line of argument is that we have to concentrate our attention on statements rather than on sentences if we are to get our ideas clear about the proper subjects of the predicates 'true' and 'false'. But this makes the task harder. A sentence-token, whether inscription or utterance, is a concrete object that can be examined and anatomized. It has parts and relations between the parts. It has semantic rules relating the parts to their meanings and syntactic rules governing the ways in which these parts can be put together. And whether it is an utterance whose parts are distinguishable sounds or an inscription composed of individual signs, it is a structured object. If we are to make any sense of a correspondence theory of truth, our best

*The token-type terminology was introduced by the American philosopher C. S. Peirce; the event-design distinction by Professor Rudolf Carnap.

hope of doing so is surely to try to relate the structure of truth-bearers, whatever these may be, to the structure of the states of affairs which they purport to describe. To shift our attention from sentences to statements is to relax our hold on this perhaps delusive thread of clarity. For we have now to ask exactly what we mean by 'statement' and in what sense, if any, statements can be truth-bearers.

We can introduce this subject by developing the distinction between sentence and statement in the way first clearly indicated by Professor Strawson.[6] We can easily see that the same type-sentence may be used in different contexts of utterance to make quite different statements. Consider sentences like:

14. He is six feet tall
15. She has blue eyes
16. It is very hot in here

And the like. They may be used with many different references in many different situations. So used they will sometimes express true statements and sometimes false ones. That is to say, the same type-sentence may be said to express different statements.

Conversely, the same statement can be made by different type-sentences. For example:

17. Brutus killed Caesar
18. Caesar was killed by Brutus
19. Mary is John's wife
20. John is Mary's husband
21. Jupiter is larger than Mars
22. Mars is smaller than Jupiter

And so on.

But what are we to count as *the same statement?* In the case of sentences we saw that there are two answers to this question of identity, depending upon whether we ask it about sentence-tokens or sentence-types. In the first case, the criterion of identity is the spatio-temporal conditions of the utterance or inscription—that S was uttered in such and such a place at this particular time, by a certain person. In the case of sentence-types, we rely on linguistic criteria, that the same words occur in the same order.

What tests of identity are available for statements? It is, of course, necessary to have such tests if we wish to say that it is statements that can be true or false. For if we do not know how to identify a statement, we can have no conception of what it would mean to say that it was true or that it was false. The examples given above to show that the same sentence may be used to make different statements use personal pronouns, adverbs of time and place like 'here' and 'now' and similar context-dependent words. We can see from this that the built-in ambiguity of such type-sentences depends on the fact that their *reference*, the features of the world to which they direct our attention, is given in the context of their utterance. But in the case of the second set of sentences (17–22) which illustrate how the same statement may be made by different type-sentences we have to ask not how the same sentence can point in different directions but how different sentences can be synonymous. This is a matter of the *sense* or *descriptive content* of a sentence and not of the direction in which it focuses our attention. This distinction between sense and reference has a long and complex history in philosophy and it can be used for several different purposes. As it is used here, it simply draws attention to distinguishable but equally necessary functions of language, to describe general features of the world and to identify points in space and time where the features are instantiated.

Consider as a rough analogy the gardener's habit of labelling plants. Walking round the grounds of the University I see an elegant tree labelled *Taxodium distichum* (Swamp Cypress). This labelling is a statement, in semi-permanent form, to the effect that the tree so labelled has a certain collection of botanical properties, namely, those assigned to the species *Taxodium distichum* by the consensus of botanists. It is a true statement so long as the label is attached to a tree of the species in question. The labelling becomes a false statement if it is detached and accidentally affixed to a tree of another species. If the label is detached and not fixed to anything, it is the equivalent of an unasserted sentence. The fixing of the label serves the two purposes of *asserting* that the labelled tree is a member of the species named and *indicating* the spot where the properties are actualized. Its *sense* is conveyed in the legend of the label; its *reference* by the place to which the label is attached.

If we grant that statements have this double function of carrying descriptive content and pointing to an occurrence of a sample of the content, we are in a better position to answer the question about the identity of statements. Clearly, we must require both identity of reference and identity of content. If two sentences however differently phrased are (a) synonymous and (b) have the same reference they are vehicles for the same statement. Thus the two sentences:

23. The victor of Marengo died in 1821
24. The deposed Emperor of France died in 1821

would not, on this criterion, express the same statement. For a descriptive content of the two sentences is different even though their reference, Napoleon, is the same.

This double criterion is, of course, not something established in the natural order of things but something postulated with the intention of bringing some order and intelligibility into our use of the concept *statement*. And it would be idle to claim that it is totally successful in this. For the concepts on which the definition depends, those of synonymy and identity of reference, are themselves unclear. We know in obvious standard cases when we have synonymy, or as much of it as is required for our purposes, and when we have identity of reference. But often we cannot know that both requisites are present in the necessary degree and so we are often in the position of doubting whether two occurrences of one sentence or of two seemingly synonymous sentences are vectors for the same statement or not. The uses of natural languages are not as straightforward as the tree-labelling model might suggest. Do the two cases in question mean exactly the same or refer to just the same space-time segment? If we cannot know this, we have no way of deciding if two assertions are assertions of the same statement.

It may be objected that to say this is to manufacture difficulties in a field already difficult enough. I have already conceded that the suggested criteria for identity of statements is not like asking of a given substance, 'Is it a conductor of electricity?' or of a certain gas, 'Do the proportions of hydrogen to carbon atoms make it butane rather than propane?' Questions of this kind are decided by the objective facts and independent of our decisions. But 'statement' is a term of everyday language taken over as a technical term in philosophy in the way that 'work' or 'power' are taken over from ordinary language to become precisely defined technical terms in physics. Unfortunately, the meanings of philosophical terms do not interlock in the way that those of physics do nor are they subject to the constraints of experimental results. Consequently they are imprecise in an irremediable way. And if we ask questions about their penumbra of imprecision, we raise doubts that are *in principle* incapable of resolution.

We can raise a further doubt about the adequacy of the notion of statement by looking more closely at the concept of *assertion*. This is one of the concepts used to distinguish statements from sentences. Part of the purpose of introducing this concept is to make the suggestion that sentences become statements and so capable of having a truth value by being asserted. And part of the function of the assertion is to give the sentence a reference, since an unasserted sentence is a mere unattached description. Such an unattached sentence occurring *in vacuo* cannot be true or false. But can this view be defended?

Assertion seems to have at least two functions. First, it is the vehicle of an utterance which is the instantiation in token form of a type-sentence. And because the utterance occurs in a particular context, that is to say, at a particular place and time, it serves to affix the descriptive content of the sentence to a particular point in the world. Secondly, it is the expression of a belief, an act which evinces a state of mind. This is important because we are apt to forget, in concentrating on sentences and utterances, that these are symbols and symbolic events. And a symbol is something which relates consciousness to some feature of the world. Were there no consciousness, there would be no symbols and so no truth or falsity.

Is assertion of a sentence then a necessary condition (if not a sufficient condition) of the sentence having a truth value? There are two objections to this that I shall consider here. (There may well be more but the following seem to me to be the important ones.) The first is that if sentences can have truth values only when they occur as asserted, it would be impossible to have a truth-functional basis to logic. If I assert as a true statement:

25. If the barometer falls half an inch in two hours, then it will rain within twelve hours

I am not *asserting* either of the separate sentences 'The barometer will fall half an inch in two hours' or 'It will rain within twelve hours'. I am merely asserting as true the conditional statement in which the first sentence is antecedent and the second is consequent. But if we therefore deny that antecedent and consequent have truth values, we deny the possibility of a truth-functional logic. However the general validity of truth-functional logic is certainly far better established than the reliability of the statement that unasserted sentences cannot have truth values. This objection, due to Professor P. T. Geach[7] is not easy to meet. Consider again the example given above:

25. If the barometer falls half an inch in the next two hours it will rain within twelve hours

Suppose that someone makes this assertion. The truth of the asserted hypothetical, according to standard logical doctrine, depends on at least one of the following two conditions being fulfilled: (A) the consequent is true; (B) the antecedent is false. Anyone who holds that only asserted sentences can have a truth value must presumably say something of the following kind: the truth of the asserted hypothetical depends on at least one of the two following conditions being fulfilled: (A') the consequent would have been true if asserted by itself; (B') the antecedent would have been false if asserted by itself.

But what does the phrase 'would have been true (or false) if asserted by itself' mean? If it means 'would not actually have a truth value until asserted' the basis of truth-functional logic is abandoned. And if it means 'does actually have a truth value which is latent until asserted' the point is yielded to Professor Geach.

The second objection is this. Indicative sentences, when uttered or otherwise instantiated, become statement-vehicles on the hypothesis that we are considering. They acquire their truth values, as we saw, from two sources: (a) from the context of their utterance, which fixes, so to speak, the sense of the sentence to a particular spatio-temporal situation; (b) from the sense of the sentence, which supplies the descriptive content of the utterance. But the second factor, the sense of the sentence, is quite independent of the first. Even to be a genuine empirical sentence, in the grammatical sense, a sentence must have such a content. And the content, as we have seen, is a necessary condition of the truth of a statement. If a sentence uttered misdescribes the situation to which it is affixed by the context of utterance, it cannot be true. But the descriptive content of a sentence is prior to its use. A sentence can express an accurate description of a certain state of affairs even if it is never applied to that state of affairs by someone who utters it. It is not just begging the question at issue to say that not all true sentences are uttered. For if they were not true in the sense of being descriptively adequate, they could not be true in the sense of being appropriately uttered.

Thus it seems no more satisfactory to postulate statements as truth-bearers than it was to choose sentences for that role. Our main reason for preferring statements to sentences, namely that sentences cannot be true or false except in a certain context of use, cannot be defended. It is even more difficult to find satisfactory criteria of identity for statements than it is for sentences. In the latter case we can at least appeal to linguistic identity and to single utterances or inscriptions, depending upon whether we are talking of types or tokens.

We are driven by these difficulties to look at the claims of a new candidate for the status of truth value vehicle—the proposition. 'Proposition' is a technical term in philosophy but in spite of its technicality it is not very well defined. There have been, in the history of philosophy, two principal meanings assigned to the term. The term '*propositio*' (and close synonyms like '*enuntiatio*') were used in medieval logic from the time of Boethius to stand for a token-sentence considered as a vehicle of meaning and, when used to express a judgement, as true or false. Some of the difficulties associated with such a use have already been discussed in connection with sentences and statements. But in more recent times, the term 'proposition' has acquired another sense. In this usage, a proposition is not a concrete thing or event such as a collection of marks on paper or a collection of sounds emitted by a speaker. It is an abstract rather than a linguistic entity, the content of a belief or the meaning of the sentence which expresses it.

There are three obvious questions prompted by such a suggestion: (a) What is the justification for it? (b) Exactly what does it mean? (c) Can it be shown that propositions, if they must be supposed to exist, can discharge the office of truth-bearer any better than sentences or statements?

(a) In answer to the first question, we could argue by elimination, pointing to the difficulties raised by alternative claimants. But there are persuasive positive arguments as well.

(i) It is a characteristic of states of consciousness that they have an object or content to which they are directed. This is true whether the state in question is one of believing, knowing, perceiving, remembering, wishing, fearing or even one of bare awareness. This object of a conscious state may not even exist in the real world as when I believe a falsehood or fear a non-existent danger. But my conscious attitude must at least have an 'intentional object' in Brentano's phrase or an 'accusative' in Ryle's. Propositions are taken to be the intentional objects of cognitive states (or acts) of mind—supposing, believing, opining, doubting, knowing and so on. That is to say, we apply the generic term 'proposition' to the objects of such states of awareness. Our assumption that there must be such objects is based on the directive character of consciousness together with the further reasons listed at (ii) to (v) below.

(ii) Knowledge, beliefs and opinions can all be communicated and so shared. They are not private in the way that my own acts of thinking and opining are private to me. If this were not so, we could not agree on any matter of fact, or, indeed disagree either. For there must be some objective content to beliefs, opinions, affirmations and conjectures if we are even to discuss them. Such objective contents are propositions.

(iii) Just as different sentences of the same language can have the same meaning, so the possibility of translation shows that the same sense can be conveyed by sentences in different languages. Such a common content of synonymous sentences, whether in the same or in different languages, is a proposition.

(iv) If propositions are to be the bearers of truth values they must be independent of human minds. For truth is not a property conferred on truth-bearers by human thinking. If P is true, it is so whether I or anyone else think of it. And if a given property (or relation) exists independently of minds, the entities in which it is instantiated must do so as well.

(v) The same proposition can be thought of at different times by the same person or by different persons and without changing its truth value. It is a fact that the battle of Waterloo took place in 1815. But the proposition expressed by

26. The battle of Waterloo took place in 1815

has no date and it makes no sense to assign it to one. A given event may be past, present or future with respect to a certain point in time. But the proposition assigning the event to the date of its occurrence must itself be timeless.

(b) Such are some of the reasons offered by philosophers who suppose that propositions are the proper subjects of the predicates 'true' and 'false'. But what are we actually claiming when we assert that there are propositions? On the basis of the reasons offered above, it seems that a proposition would be an entity with the following properties: (i) it is immaterial and not locatable in space and time although it can make appearances, as it were, on the physical stage embodied in words; (ii) it is independent of any particular mind and of minds in general although it is a public object which can be contemplated by a mind; (iii) it is neutral between languages although when embodied in an utterance it must be expressed in some particular natural language.

Such objects, if they exist, are strange and unfamiliar, though that is no good reason for refusing to admit their existence if reliable arguments require it. They are clearly the same sort of entity as Plato's Forms or Ideas and indeed are supported by similar arguments. Plato's Forms were invoked to explain the objectivity and reliability of knowledge; propositions are hypothesized to provide a subject for the predicate 'true'. The history of philosophy since Plato has shown that it is possible to give an adequate account of most kinds of knowledge without recourse to belief in the Forms. Some philosophers of mathematics, it is true, would still count themselves as Platonists as regards numbers and perhaps some other mathematical entities. But as we have already agreed to restrict attention to *empirical* hypotheses in examining the correspondence theory of truth, we need not concern ourselves further with questions proper to the philosophy of mathematics.

One objection which has been raised against this account of propositions by Professor Ryle[8] should be examined here. (Ryle offered the argument not as a conclusive refutation of the theory but as weakening the argument from the intentionality of consciousness.) It is supposed that minds can be acquainted with propositions which can stand for or represent or correspond to *facts*. But either we can know the facts directly and so have no need of propositions to represent them to us; or we cannot know them directly and then can never know if the propositions represent the facts adequately or even, presumably, if there are any facts to be represented. Thus if propositions can perform their hypothesized task, they are superfluous; and if they cannot, they are useless.

Similar arguments are well known in other parts of the theory of knowledge, in particular, in connection with the causal theory of perception. But however effective the argument may be against a representative theory of perception, it is quite ineffective against propositions. The supporter of propositions may well admit that we do sometimes know facts directly; but not always. Then the proposition may serve as a clue to the unknown fact. Suppose, for example, that a geologist entertains the proposition, 'There is an oilfield beneath the Bristol Channel.' Examination of the consequences of the hypothesized proposition may lead to the discovery of the oilfield. In this case, consideration of the proposition will have led to discovery of the fact. Thus propositions can be useful surrogates for states of affairs, either as clues to yet unknown facts or as *aides-mémoire* to facts experienced in the past. But both propositions and facts are accessible to our consciousness. In this, they are quite unlike physical objects which, on the representative theory of perception, hide forever behind a veil of sense data.

(c) Can we test this hypothesis by seeing whether it performs its office of providing satisfactory truth-bearers? One way of testing it is to raise some questions about these hypothetical intentional objects. First, are they supposed to be true or false *in themselves* or are they, like sentences, true or false only as they are used in making assertions? The answer to this must presumably be that the first alternative is the correct one. They are not like labels that we may select and then apply, correctly or incorrectly, to bits of the environment. They carry in their own natures an implicit reference to those concrete features of the world that make them true.

Suppose then that a proposition is false. We must be prepared to suppose this; for if propositions are to be truth-bearers, they must be vehicles of falsehood as well. Indeed, for every one true proposition, there will be an uncountable multitude of false ones. To take a specific example, I am now looking at the piece of green stone on the table in front of me. The token-sentence:

13. There is a piece of green stone on the table

is a verbal instantiation of the proposition which truly reflects the state of affairs that I am observing. But the sentences:

27. There is no piece of stone on the table
28. There is a piece of red stone on the table
29. There is a piece of black stone on the table
30. There is a rat on the table

(and so on indefinitely) are all verbalizations of their corresponding *false* propositions. Most of such false propositions will never be entertained by a human mind, as being too bizarre and improbable to merit even fleeting consideration. Surely the hypothesis is beginning to overpopulate our intentional universe to the point of pollution. Such teeming hordes of false propositions serve no purpose except to satisfy the logical exigencies of the hypothesis that suggests them. This is not indeed a conclusive reason for saying that propositions do not exist; but it is a very good reason for not supposing that they do.

Secondly, we may raise questions about the connections between propositions and language. The hypothesis that we are considering suggests that propositions are mind-independent intentional objects which can be crystallized, so to speak, in verbal form. Now it is an important feature of natural language that the sentence-tokens by which we assert propositions are never completely specific. The sentence:

13. There is a piece of green stone on the table

is compatible with an indefinitely large number of alternative states of affairs. It could be true of any one of them (in the sense of 'true' in which sentences can be said to be true). It could be true of many different tables at many different times and of many different pieces of stone. We can, of course, narrow its range of possible reference by suitably filling out its points of vagueness. For example:

> 31. There is (at 11.35 a.m. BST on 22 November 1971) a piece of green quartz weighing exactly 72·64 grammes on the table situated in Room 231 of Queen's Building, Exeter University

Even here, of course, there are several possible points of ambiguity. But we like to suppose that these could, in principle (as we say), be removed.

Whether this is possible is a point to which I shall return later when we come to discuss Professor Quine's hypothesis of *eternal sentences*. For the moment, I want to look at the consequences of this for the relation between propositions and language. Since propositions are, by supposition, true or false they must be completely specific in their detail and reference. Were this not so, the same proposition might be true of an indefinitely large number of states of affairs. Indeed, the same proposition might be true of situation S_1 and false of S_2 simply because its lack of specificity permitted the ambiguous reference. But if this is so, it is clear that nearly all declarative sentences *cannot* adequately express propositions; for very few, if any, sentences are so exactly qualified that they can refer to one and only one state of affairs.

Thus the relation between propositions and language becomes not a one-one relation of proposition to sentence but a one-many relation. The same proposition can be expressed (i) in different languages, (ii) in synonymous sentences of the same language and (iii) in different sentences of the same language which differ in degrees of descriptive and referential precision. And in the light of (iii), the truth of our assertions and communications becomes a matter of degree. For truth may reside primarily (on this hypothesis) in propositions. But secondarily it resides in the linguistic expressions which we use to record, express, consider and communicate propositions. Propositions are indeed on this view simply the cognitive content of declarative sentences which convey this content with varying degrees of completeness and precision.

If this is the case, it raises a serious doubt about the usefulness and indeed the point of postulating propositions to be the vehicles of truth values. We saw that if a sentence is unasserted, in some contexts at least, it cannot be said to have a truth value. (For example, a sentence used simply as a grammatical example can hardly be said to be true or false.) Why then should a proposition be credited with a truth value so long as it does not form the content (or part of the content) of some assertion? The point can be put in the form of a dilemma. If a proposition is no more than the cognitive content of a possible assertion, it is hard to see how it can serve the function of a truth-bearer. And if it does have a truth value quite independent of any assertive use to which it may be put, it is hard to see the difference between a proposition and a possible state of affairs. A true proposition will then be an actual state of affairs; a false proposition will be a possible but unactualized state of affairs. This is indeed an interpretation of the term which has appealed to some philosophers. Carnap, for example,[9] says: 'It is used neither for a linguistic expression nor for a subjective mental occurrence, but rather for something objective that may or may not be exemplified in nature.' And Henry Leonard, in a well known textbook of logic[10] defines a proposition as 'a logically possible situation or state of affairs'.

Such definitions have the great advantage of making the term intelligible but only at the cost of making it useless for the correspondence theory of truth. For the two terms which are somehow supposed on that theory to stand in the relation of correspondence are collapsed into one. 'True' and 'false' are now interpreted as 'actual' and 'possible but unactualized'; and they refer to states of affairs and not to beliefs and their symbolic expression. This is certainly out of accord with our commonsense pre-analytic concepts of truth and falsity and violates Russell's second condition for a satisfactory analysis of truth. Truth and falsity become, on this interpretation, objective properties of the world which are quite independent of our knowledge and beliefs. Whether or not the account of truth which follows from this view of propositions is acceptable must be argued at greater length. It is at least clear that the correspondence theory of truth is not to be sustained on such a premiss.

Some recent developments in linguistics have offered a basis for a suggestion about the nature of propositions which may do something to make the concept more acceptable. The distinction between the *deep structure* and the *surface structure* of language can be traced to the work of Wilhelm von Humboldt in the early nineteenth century and even earlier to the Port Royal grammarians of the seventeenth century.[11] But for contemporary linguistics the concept seems to have originated in the work of Professor C. H. Hockett published in 1958.[12] It was developed by Professor Noam Chomsky and is now well established as a basic concept in transformational generative grammar (and elsewhere in contemporary linguistic theory). The basic idea of a generative grammar, due to Chomsky, is that it is a set of rules which will suffice to generate all (and only) the grammatical sentences of a language. By 'grammatical' sentences here is meant those sentences which would be accepted as grammatical by native speakers. Although no such grammar has so far been completely worked out for any natural language, very considerable progress has been made in the few years since Chomsky's theories were formulated.

Obvious grounds for the distinction between deep structure and surface structure arise from the fact that we can all recognize both synonymous sentences and ambiguous sentences in our own native language. For example:

32. Someone gave the child a knife
33. Someone gave a knife to the child
34. The child was given a knife
35. A knife was given to the child

would all be accepted as synonymous sentences in English. The surface structure (that is, the actual words used in the order in which they occur) of 32 to 35 is different in each case. But they might be said by a philosopher to mean the same in virtue of expressing the *same proposition*, or by a linguist of the transformational school to have the same deep structure. This deep structure is not an actual verbal expression but an abstract entity which can be given an artificial symbolic expression in a form such as:

36. Someone-past-give-a knife-to-the child

or, more vividly, by a tree diagram as shown on p. 51. This structure can be converted, by transformational rules, into any one of 32 to 35.

Conversely, consider the following sentence:

37. Starving prisoners would be cruel

This could obviously be read as:

38. It would be cruel to starve prisoners

or as

39. Prisoners, who are starving, would be cruel

Appropriate deep structures corresponding to 38 and 39 would be convertible by transformational rules to a common surface structure, as in 37.

Some linguists have suggested that there are deep structures common to different languages; indeed, that all intertranslatable sentences, in whatever language they may appear in their surface structure dress, might have a common deep structure. This suggestion is at present no more than an unfalsified hypothesis. But it gives some ground for supposing that there is a strong link, perhaps even an equivalence, between the deep structure of an indicative sentence and a proposition in the sense of an objective intentional entity. If that is the case, we could look to future developments in linguistics to clarify the concept of proposition and augment its acceptability by linking a technical term in philosophy with a central concept in the empirical science of language. Indeed, Chomsky in a recent essay on the subject[13] has linked the two terms. 'We can thus distinguish the *surface structure* of the sentence, the organisation into categories and phrases that is directly associated with the physical signal, from the underlying *deep structure*, also a system of categories and phrases, but with a more abstract character. Thus the surface structure of the sentence "A wise man is honest" might analyze it into the subject "a wise man" and the predicate "is honest". The deep structure, however, will be rather different. It will, in particular, extract from the complex idea that constitutes the subject of the surface structure an underlying proposition with the subject "man" and the predicate "be wise". In fact, the deep structure, in the traditional view, is a system of two propositions, neither of which is asserted, but which interrelate in such a way as to express the meaning of the sentence "a wise man is honest".'

Chomsky goes on to illustrate the deep structure by a formula and a tree diagram. The diagram (in which read S = sentence,

NP = noun phrase, VP = verb phrase according to the usual convention) is as follows:

40.

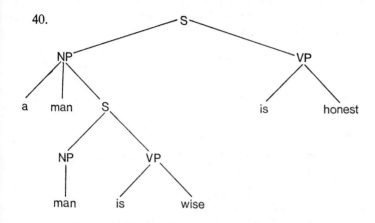

This shows how the two unasserted propositions occur in the deep structure of the original sentence. The fact that this structure is no longer linear or one-dimensional is of some importance, as will be seen later. Here again, of course, we meet the same difficulty that we have met before; namely, in what sense can unasserted propositions, even when they form part of an assertion be said to have truth values? This is no more and no less a problem for the hypothesis that a proposition is the deep structure of a sentence than it was for the supposition that sentences are truth-bearers.

Philosophers of an empiricist tradition have difficulty in accepting the existence of abstract entities, such as propositions are supposed to be, on either or both of two grounds. In the first place, they are not objects of direct experience but inferred entities. And they are not inferred entities of a scientifically respectable kind like genes and electrons. For the hypotheses that genes or electrons exist can be used to predict observable consequences whose occurrence will serve to confirm the hypothesis. This is not the case with propositions, nor do they, like inferred scientific entities, fit into and fill out the structure of a science. They are postulated merely *ad hoc*, to meet the supposed exigencies of a philosophical argument.

But this puritanism about abstract objects is difficult to maintain consistently. Even strict empiricists admit numbers to their universe. And we can make the same kind of distinction between the abstract X and its temporary materializations with regard to plays, symphonies or even cookery recipes as we do with propositions and their corresponding sentences. It is indeed possible to give a nominalistic account of such things just as it is possible in the case of propositions. But on the whole, even the most austere empiricists have not thought it worth their while, so far as I know, to try to explain cookery recipes, chemical formulae, doctors' prescriptions and the like in terms of classes of their actual realizations.

The second ground for rejecting abstract intentional objects is an appeal to the principle of intellectual economy attributed to William of Ockham—Ockham's razor, as it has been called. '*Entia non sunt multiplicanda praeter necessitatem*' could be read in this context as 'No unnecessary hypotheses'. It may be that the hypothesis of the existence of objective propositions is open to criticism on the grounds that we have considered. But as long as no other hypothesis will provide truth-bearers, it might be deemed necessary however strange and difficult to understand. A plausible alternative has however been offered by Professor W. V. Quine.[14] Contrast the following two sentences:

41. The prime minister is overweight
42. The benzene molecule has six carbon atoms

42 is true of all benzene molecules at all times and places; but the truth of 41 depends on which prime minister we are referring to and when we make the assertion. But we can fill in the details of 41 so that its truth value is immune to the variations introduced by ambiguous reference. Thus:

43. The prime minister of England at 30 September 1971 is overweight

43 will be timelessly true or false, provided that we have removed all vagueness and ambiguity. If we do this with all indicative sentences, we shall have sentences whose truth values 'stay fixed through time and from speaker to speaker'. Such sentences, with permanently fixed truth values, Quine calls 'eternal sentences'. They are such as to 'stay forever true, or forever false, independent

of any special circumstances under which they happen to be uttered or written'.[15] They must of course be type-sentences and not tokens. As Quine explains: 'A sentence is not an event of utterance, but a universal: a repeatable sound pattern or repeatedly approximable norm.'[16]

Mathematical and logical truths are the most obvious candidates for the status of 'eternal sentence'. Indeed, they have been traditionally known as 'eternal truths' since the time of Leibniz. But we are concerned only with empirical truth. And it may well be doubted if all empirical statements can be shown to be expressible in such a form that their truth values are timelessly fixed.

We use many indicative sentences whose verbal expressions are of uncertain reference. But in the great majority of such cases, ambiguity is removed by the context of their utterance. A sentence like

44. I noticed that he was there at the time.

taken by itself, leaves us uncertain about the reference to 'I', 'he', 'there' and 'at the time'. But when it is uttered in a conventional context, we are in no doubt about the place, time and persons referred to. If the context does leave us in doubt about any feature of the reference, we can remove uncertainty by replacing pronouns by proper names or descriptions. For example, in 44 we can replace 'he' by 'John' or by 'John Smith' or 'the tall man with red hair' or something of the kind. But can we always do this so that we have an eternal sentence available for every situation that we have to describe?

There are two sources of indefinite reference in natural languages: first, the indicator terms available do not uniquely identify the exact space-time location of the situation sketched by our descriptive terms; secondly, the descriptive terms are essentially general. That is to say, it is the nature of descriptive terms that they are capable of being applied correctly to an indefinitely large number of individuals. Now the point of postulating eternal sentences is to have truth-bearers which are context-neutral. Whenever or wherever such a sentence is uttered or written it must contain, *within itself*, the means of uniquely identifying the fact which it unambiguously describes. Let us consider some of the difficulties raised by this requirement.

(a) Although the hypothesis of eternal sentences was introduced to avoid having to suppose the existence of propositions, it is noteworthy that some of the difficulties that make us willing to abandon propositions can also be used to discredit eternal sentences.

(i) The objection that propositions are Platonic entities and open to the well-known difficulties of a Platonic metaphysics can equally well be used against eternal sentences. For they are not tokens, concrete events of utterance or particular inscriptions, but types, that is to say, patterns of utterance which are, as Quine admits, universals. (It should be added that Quine's rejection of the traditional propositions is based not on any dislike for Platonic metaphysics but on scruples about the possibility of genuine synonymy between sentences in natural languages.) However, such objections as may be offered to the postulation of universals apply to eternal sentences as much as to propositions.

(ii) We saw that to assume the existence of propositions populates the universe with an uncountable multitude of objective falsehoods. To the extent that this counts as an objection to the postulation of propositions it must count equally against eternal sentences. For there must be eternal false sentences which uniquely identify all those logically possible states of affairs which are never brought to actuality. Indeed, to every true E-sentence (as we may call them for short) there will correspond an indefinite swarm of false E-sentences. (It will be remembered that there was an analogous embarrassment of riches with propositions.) Doubtless there is no reason to suppose that the universe is constructed according to the law of parsimony. But such consequences of a hypothesis make us feel uneasy about accepting it unless logic compels us. We might indeed evade the consequence by assuming a deterministic universe in which there could be no unactualized possibilities. But this is a very radical remedy which has disadvantages of its own. So far then it might be said that the hypothesis of eternal sentences has little to offer that we cannot obtain by accepting propositions. The only clear gain seems to be that E-sentences, being linguistic entities, have a familiar and comprehensible *structure*. The sense in which propositions have a structure is difficult to elucidate unless we make them useless for correspondence by equating them with facts.

(b) We may ask about E-sentences another question that was raised about propositions: when we say that they are truth-bearers, do we mean that they are true or false *in themselves* and independent of any use to which they may be put in acts of assertion? Or do we mean that they are capable of bearing truth but actually do so only when used to refer to a state of affairs for which they are fitted by their cognitive content? (For example, a two-ton lorry is capable of carrying goods to the weight of two tons but is not always used in this way.) In Quine's use of the term, the first alternative is correct. But for this to be a feasible alternative, it is necessary that indicative sentences in natural languages are always capable of being filled out by suitable indicators and specifiers so that the combination of their indicative and descriptive force locks the sentence uniquely to its corresponding fact or (if it is a false sentence) fails to attach it to any actually existing state of affairs. We can best investigate this possibility by examining an example. Let us look again at:

13. There is a piece of green stone on the table

For this to be transformed into an occurrence of a true eternal sentence, we have (i) to specify exactly the time and place to which the sentence refers and (ii) describe the piece of stone with sufficient precision for the sentence to describe this *and only this* state of affairs. Clearly 13 does not satisfy this condition. For even if we amplify the sentence to identify the exact time and place referred to, this will not make it a completely context-free sentence. The descriptive phrase 'green stone' would still apply to an indefinitely large number of possibilities, only one of which was actualized. For example, if the colour of the stone is jade green, 13 would still accurately fit the case where the stone was emerald green; and so on. Only if we could specify in language the exact size, shape, colour, chemical structure and so on of the individual referred to could the amended version of 13 be a token of the required eternal sentence. Otherwise it would be *at the same time* a token of a sentence fitting an indefinitely large number of possible but unactualized states of affairs. And so, contrary to the hypothesis we are considering, it would be false as well as true.

This is an inevitable consequence of the nature of language. The descriptive lexicon of a language forms a net whose mesh is small enough to catch those qualitative features of the world that we find useful. A smaller mesh (from a richer lexicon) would preserve still smaller variations of quality. But no language is rich enough to mirror exactly the features of the world it describes. For the world is a world of individuals; and language to serve its function must be irremediably general. This consequence is, of course, a corollary of Quine's requirement that eternal sentences can be false as well as true. But if these sentences are indeed to be genuine vehicles of truth values, it is hard to see how this stipulation can be dispensed with.

(c) The foregoing argument against the possibility of eternal sentences is based on the essential generality of descriptive terms. But a similar point can be made about the indicator words which tie a given description to a particular place and time. As space and time are continuous,* no point, interval, area or volume can be uniquely distinguished by a numerical measurement. An 'exact' measurement can be exact only within conventional or explicit limits of error. For example, if 10 centimetres means, let us say, 10cm $\pm$ ·01cm, the measurement admits a *class* of possible lengths which would satisfy it. If it does not, it is meaningless since there is no procedure of measurement which can identify *exactly* one unique quantity from a continuous medium. So our hypothetical eternal sentence would be a variable which could be satisfied by any one of an indefinite range of states of affairs. And again it would be both true and false, contrary to hypothesis.

(d) The switch from propositions which are neutral between particular languages to eternal sentences which are grammatical constructions of a particular language raises problems. It is an empirical fact about languages that they are intertranslatable. No doubt, as Quine has emphasized, there are reasonable doubts about the limits of exactness with which cognitive content can be conveyed from one language to another. But no one doubts that some transfer is possible. And it seems an objection to the hypothesis that eternal sentences are the only truth-bearers that equivalent sentences in different languages can be equivalent in virtue of a common cognitive content without that content itself having a truth value. Let us suppose, waiving the objections

*This seems a reasonable assumption. But conceivably it might be false.

outlined above, that eternal sentences are possible and that S_1 is such a sentence in English which is true of a certain state of affairs A and let S_2 and S_3 be sentences in Chinese and Turkish which are also true of A. Since S_1, S_2 and S_3 have a common cognitive content C in virtue of which they are mutually inter-translatable, why may we not say that C is true of A? Indeed, C here seems just to be a proposition in a slightly different guise with the same advantages and drawbacks that we have already considered. Thus even if eternal sentences were possible (and we may well doubt that they are) they do not seem to enable us to dispense with propositions. And since this was the main point of postulating such sentences, the hypothesis loses its purpose. Whether the hypothesis is required at all depends on whether we accept Quine's arguments about the indeterminacy of translation and the difficulties involved in the concept of synonymy.[17] But even if we do accept these views, it cannot be denied that languages are *to some degree* intertranslatable. The common cognitive content requisite for this is all we need to reintroduce propositions and so to render the hypothesis of eternal sentences unnecessary.

(e) It is an important fact about eternal sentences (and one of the reasons for Quine's rejection of propositions in their favour) that they are specific to a language. But it is possible for the same series of sounds (or the same set of inscriptions in the same order) to instantiate a true sentence in language A and a false one in language B. This is so whether languages A and B are (i) two stages of development of the same language or (ii) two different languages. As an instance of (i) consider:

45. Eve was coy and buxom

said in Chaucer's time and in the reign of Victoria. This might be true at one time, when 'coy and buxom' meant, in modern English 'quiet and submissive' and false later.* As an instance of (ii) consider:

46. *Han var rolig*

said at a funeral about the deceased by a Dane and a Swede, each speaking in his own language. Since the word '*rolig*' means 'quiet'

---

*Other examples of common English words which have changed their meaning with this consequence are 'nice', 'silly', 'dangerous' and 'curious'.

in Danish and 'lively and entertaining' in Swedish, 46 could represent sentences with different truth values in the two languages. But it is necessary for eternal sentences, as the only genuine truth-vehicles, to be unambiguous. It will therefore be necessary to label each eternal sentence, in a meta-language, with the name of the language of which it is a sentence and the stage of development of that language. And what if the meta-language is ambiguous as well?*

There are other arguments that one might adopt in criticism of Quine's hypothesis but it is unnecessary to pursue the matter. We have looked at several aspirants for the status of truth-bearer —beliefs, judgements, sentences, statements, utterances, propositions, eternal sentences. Each has its own advantages and drawbacks. In such a situation we have to choose the alternative with the fewest and least decisive failings. On the arguments we have looked at so far, beliefs, in the sense of the contents of occurrent belief acts, seem to be most immune to criticism. But before this question can be pursued further, we have to look at facts, the other term of the supposed relation of correspondence. We must then examine the nature of the relation itself.

---

*Quine is not, of course, unaware of this possibility but he offers no conclusive way round the difficulty.[18]

7 | Facts

It might be said that we all know what a fact is. No doubt this is true at a commonsense or 'pre-analytic' level of discourse. But if we are to examine the thesis that true beliefs or statements correspond to facts, we need to elucidate the concept a little. Fortunately, examination of this term of the relation will not take nearly so long as our survey of potential truth-bearers. For the status of truth-donor we have only one candidate to examine— *facts* or *states of affairs*.

Little purpose is served by offering a definition of 'fact'. Of the few philosophers who have attempted a definition, Russell (following McTaggart)[19] said that he meant by a fact 'that a certain thing has a certain quality or that certain things have a certain relation'. But as 'quality' and 'relation' are technical philosophical terms and 'fact' is not, such definitions, though they may be helpful in suitable contexts, do little to clarify the concept. We will do better by accepting our vague pre-analytic notion and trying to distinguish facts from non-facts and different types of fact from each other. We may take as a premiss of the correspondence theory that facts are truth-donors or, in Russell's phrase, 'those features of the constitution of the world which make our assertions true (if they are true) or false (if they are false)'.[20] But this presupposition is not, at least at this stage of our discussion, in any way elucidatory of the notion of fact. It merely emphasizes that facts are objective features of the world and so independent of minds and their activities. Whether even this presumption can be defended remains to be seen.

The world can be looked at and described in many different ways. It is a collection of things, a collection of qualities and a collection of events. We could imagine a set of cosmic catalogues, compiled by the recording angel, in which the universe was listed from these different points of view. But things, qualities (including, of course, relational qualities) or events are not facts although they are, so to speak, ingredients of facts. My tie is a thing and its colour is a quality. But we say that it is a fact that my tie is blue. A piece of litmus paper is a thing and its blue colour is a quality. The change of quality from blue to red when the litmus paper is immersed in acid is an event. That the paper turned from blue to red is a fact. Doubtless there could be no facts if there were no things, qualities and events. But it is facts (or states of affairs) that are truth-donors, not their ingredients.

One of the most obvious differences between facts and their ingredients (and, on reflection, one of the most puzzling) is that whereas things, qualities and events are immersed in the world of space and time, facts are somehow frozen and abstracted from the spatio-temporal continuum. That continuum, indeed, consists of a web of events which in turn consist of individual things changing their properties and their relations to other things. Things exist in space and endure through time; qualities are instantiated at different points of space and at different times; events occur at particular places and times. But facts are not located in space, nor do they endure through time. The battle of Marengo took place on 14 June 1800. But the fact that the battle of Marengo took place on that date is not something which has a place or a date. At 1 January 1800 the battle of Marengo was a future event; but the fact that the battle took place on 14 June of that year was not a future fact at 1 January. For facts are time-less and it makes no sense to talk of them as past, present or future.

Let us suppose that someone were to challenge this last statement in the following way: 'You say that facts are timeless and that it makes no sense to talk of them as past, present or future. But what is the evidence for this statement? It cannot be an empirical statement; for evidence for empirical statements is observation of occurrences that take place in space and time. And you cannot pretend that you have searched for facts all over the world and failed to find them as a romantic zoologist might have searched for unicorns. Nor can it be a statement of logic; for if it were, it could be proved deductively. And no one has ever proved it. Therefore it can be no more than a proposal for a philosophical convention that we are free, as we are with all conventions, to accept or reject as we please.'

To such an objector the answer is that we are proposing a convention. But, like many conventions, it has an important point. The place and date of an event is intrinsic to it. That is to say, the point in time and the place of its occurrence helps to make it the event that it is. (For example, it fixes its place in the causal network.) But dating a fact is pleonastic. To say that it is a fact now (in England in 1972) that the battle of Marengo took place on 14 June 1800 is like saying that two plus three will make five in Japan in 1986 or that carbon atoms had six protons in Holland in 1738. Such specifications are pointless because they are empty of information. This is the justification for speaking of facts as being timeless and having no location in space. It is vacuous as well as uneconomic and misleading to do otherwise.

This convention is a sensible one but it has its dangers. We have already seen that part of the problem in accepting propositions as truth vehicles is that it is difficult to put any meaning into the condition that they are subsistent entities which are independent alike of minds and of the physical world. We have seen too that to regard facts in such a way offers a temptation to equate them with propositions, a temptation to which some philosophers have yielded. If we are to say that facts are somehow independent of the world of space and time, we have nevertheless to give an account of them that will not betray us into a Platonic metaphysics on the one hand, or abandon the notion of correspondence on the other.

There is clearly a very close connection between facts and events. How are we to explain this while, on the one hand, we maintain the distinction between events as spatio-temporal and facts as free of space-time context and, on the other, refuse to let facts evanesce into propositions? Perhaps the simplest way of explaining both the distinction and the relationship between them is to say that facts and events are the same objects regarded from different points of view. We are ourselves objects immersed in the space-time continuum and very naturally look at and describe features of that continuum in their context of spatio-temporal relations. Past, present and future are, for many of our purposes, categories of immediate concern. When we think and talk in this way, we think and talk of events. But we are also semi-rational creatures who have an innate interest in sorting out our world into its regular patterns of recurrence and co-existence and in predicting and controlling nature through our knowledge. This requires setting ourselves, in imagination, outside the flux of events and regarding the world as a static pattern viewed *sub specie aeternitatis*. From this viewpoint, we look on events as fixed in their spatio-temporal positions, that is to say, we interpret the world as a world of facts. As animals, we interest ourselves in events; as rational beings, in facts.

Part of the difficulty of establishing the distinction and the connection between events and facts is the necessity of using a language in which the tenses of verbs are a pervasive feature. Ideally the language in which we talk of facts should be a tenseless language in which the time reference (and of course the space reference too) is provided by dates and place names. Tensed expressions implicitly set the user at a point in time from which he categorizes the event referred to as past, present or future. Compare:

47. The F.A. Cup Final in 1972 will take place at Wembley on 6 May

with:

48. The F.A. Cup Final *take place* (tenseless verb) at Wembley on 6 May 1972

47 is (as written today) a prediction of a future event. After the event it will be rephrased as a record and expressed in the past tense. 48 on the contrary is a statement of fact whose nature is best brought out by this somewhat ungrammatical locution. So formulated, it can be made at any time.

So far, we have talked as though facts were simply frozen events. But the notion of an event is a vague one. The standard cases of events are physical changes which happen sufficiently fast to be observed as changes and which are of sufficient interest to us to be noticed or commented on. Flashes of lightning, earthquakes, births, deaths, battles, revolutions—any of these would count as events. But the growth and decay of a plant or of a star happen too slowly to qualify. It is easy to represent a slow process, like the growth of a plant, as an event by speeding up a film of a selection of its successive stages. From considerations of this kind, we can see that the distinction between an event and any other process of change is an arbitrary one. The standard cases of events are changes which are both swift and interesting. But the differences between these standard cases and other changes, however slow and boring, are merely matters of degree. So too it is a matter of convention where we place the beginning and end of an event. We carve out a section from a continuous process of change and give it a label—a lightning flash, an earthquake, a battle, a death—and so on. And in doing so, we are merely highlighting features of special interest in a continuum of change.

How does this affect the relationship between events and facts? The relation seems to be, not so much that facts are frozen events, as that they are dated slices of a continuous process. Given that a certain process has stages $S_1, S_2 \ldots S_n$ we tag a certain stage, say S_k, as worthy of note for some reason and say: It is a fact that S_k took place at t_k. But any other discriminable stage of the process could equally well be sliced and dated in the same way. So facts are frozen and dated slices of events. In this form they are packaged conveniently for our comprehension.

Such at least are facts of one type, particular facts, as they are sometimes called. But not all our beliefs are about particular facts. Many are concerned with generalities, causal relationships, natural kinds or statistical regularities. These are facts which match, in some way still to be clarified, our beliefs about them when these beliefs are true. For example, it is a fact that carbon atoms have six protons, that species evolve through the mechanisms of natural selection, that human intelligence is genetically controlled, that carbon monoxide is poisonous to mammals—and so on. Such facts are not the outcome of slicing processes of change synchronically, so to speak, across the grain. Rather they are the features of the world that we detect by dissecting natural processes diachronically along the time dimension. Such facts do not contain identifying dates but represent persistent natural trends or patterns. They are manifested through time and can be at best exemplified at any particular point of it. We can call them, following Russell, general facts. The phrase covers a large and very heterogeneous class.

Do particular and general facts together cover the class of truth-donors? Here we face a difficulty that we have already glanced at in connection with propositions and with eternal sentences. If we require that facts are to be truth-donors, must we also say that they are sources of falsity when our beliefs are mistaken?

It will be remembered that we accepted as one of Russell's three conditions for a satisfactory theory of truth that the theory must also account for error. Indeed, if it was not for the prevalence of error we should hardly be concerned to work out an adequate account of the nature of truth. Moreover, many of our beliefs, both true and false, embody *denials* rather than affirmations. I believe that the carbon atom does *not* have five protons or seven or any other number than six. And so on for all my other beliefs. For every true affirmation we can make an indefinitely large number of true denials. And, on the supposition that true affirmations are backed by facts, what are we to suppose that true denials are true of? Moreover, for every true assertion that we make, there is a corresponding false denial formed by negating the assertion. What are we to say is the source of the truth value *false* in these cases?

The natural answer to this question is that true denials (or negative affirmations) are made true by negative facts; and correspondingly, false assertions are rendered false by their matching negative facts. As Russell once argued, 'A thing cannot be false except because of a fact, so that you find it extremely difficult to say what happens when you make a positive assertion that is false, unless you are going to admit negative facts.'[21] But if we pursue the consequences of this supposition, we meet the same kind of unwelcome extravagance of hypothetical entities that made propositions and eternal sentences look so unplausible. Let us take a concrete example. I look at the carpet before me which is empty of any animal life. I can say truly:

49. There is no dog on the carpet

This is a true statement and on the supposition that we are entertaining, it is true in virtue of a negative fact, namely, that there is no dog there. But I could have made an indefinitely large number of other true statements by substituting for the word 'dog' the name of any other species of animal, real or mythical. Are we seriously to suppose that each of that multitude of true statements is rendered veridical by its corresponding negative fact? Such a proposal seems no more than a metaphysical extravaganza. After all, what are the observable facts (in the straightforward everyday sense of the word 'fact')? Simply that the carpet is empty. It is clear that even a tepid concern for intellectual economy must lead us to question the postulation of negative facts if there is any more plausible way of accounting for the truth of such familiar statements.

It may be helpful here to look back at the reasons which led us to introduce facts at all into our analysis of the nature of truth and falsity. Truth-bearers, whatever they may be, receive their truth values from some feature of the world that is objective and independent of our thoughts and beliefs. It was to these features that we gave their commonplace name of 'facts'. It was their supposed function to be the donors of truth and falsity to our beliefs, statements or whatever we agree to assign as truth-vehicles. Now it must be noticed here that this essential function of being a truth-donor cannot be carried out by anything that is not an objective and independent part of the world which would retain its nature whether or not there were any minds or symbolic systems and whether or not, in consequence, there were any truth values. But have we not already, in what we have been saying about facts, compromised that essential character on which their truth-donating capacity depends?

To talk or think about these matters, we are compelled to make use of language. And in using language about any feature of the world we have to conceptualize what we talk about. Negation is a linguistic device which we use for our conceptual convenience. There is nothing in the world of brute fact which corresponds to negation. There is just a shifting pattern of things, qualities and relations, a kaleidoscope of presences and absences of things and properties. Some states of affairs exclude others; to use a term of Leibniz, some facts are not *compossible* with certain other facts. It is these absences and exclusions that we use negation to designate. But these absences and exclusions are not themselves features of the world and so not themselves the components of facts. It is just that some of them interest us for various reasons and so we have an artifice of language to focus attention on them. To negate a statement is just to affirm that nature is otherwise than we might conceive it to be. But objective reality has no gaps in it, though it may have features that are not compossible with what we note as absent by our use of negation. So there are no negative facts. By reaching this conclusion we do something to refrain from conceptualizing truth-donors to a degree which would incapacitate them for their function.

C

But can we really refrain from conceptualizing facts? And if we cannot, do we have to abandon the correspondence of truth in all its forms? It is a well known objection to these accounts of truth and one which has been especially emphasized by its idealist critics, that we cannot in any way experience, still less understand, the world unless we put the facets of our experience into conceptual pigeonholes. Once we do that, the world of fact, (if there is such a world) retreats beyond our cognitive reach. What we compare and relate in arriving at true conclusions is not beliefs with facts but two conceptual systems, one of our judgements and the other of experience but crystallized into conceptual form.

In order to do what we can to answer this objection, we have first of all to appreciate its full force. In what we have already said about facts, we have admitted that our notion of a fact is of some already intellectualized feature of the world, extracted from its concrete context, sliced and dated and packaged in language for our cognitive convenience. Though our denial of negative facts did something to mitigate a conceptual taint in truth-donors, there are still other arguments to be examined. Let us take a concrete example. I am now looking out of a window into a garden. I can see a lawn, a bird table, various birds (chaffinches, greenfinches, nuthatches and others), a tulip tree, camellia and azalea bushes—and so on. The contents of my observation could be re-stated in a list of facts: 'There is a greenfinch at such and such a place'; and the like. Now even if I do not record by observations in language but simply contemplate the scene in an attitude of aesthetic detachment, I am still contemplating a scene which has been ordered and classified according to my conceptual scheme. If this were not so, the contents of my visual field would represent merely a shifting patchwork of colour and not a garden scene with trees, birds and so on.

We can easily appreciate this, if we set someone to look out on this scene who has not had the opportunity of acquiring a conceptual scheme similar to my own. Let us take, as an extreme example but one which makes the point clearly, the case of an adult blind from birth from congenital cataract who has just recently had the cataracts removed by surgery and so can now 'see'. I put the word in quotes because, as has been amply established by observation of such cases,[22] the patient will 'see' only a shifting patchwork of colour which will be meaningless to him in visual terms. He will not see trees, grass, birds and so on as I do, until he has learned slowly and painfully over several months to interpret the contents of this visual field conceptually. So too a new-born baby, a savage from central New Guinea, an Eskimo, a dog or a bird, would all have substantially* the same material in their visual field if set before this scene. But the facts open to their observation would be very different and would vary according to the concepts they had previously acquired. And these concepts would vary with innate capacity for concept formation, innate or acquired interests and so on. (The new-born infant would, of course, be totally without concepts of any kind.) It is considerations of this kind which make the idealist argument a very strong one at first sight. The conclusion that we are asked to accept is this: on the correspondence theory of truth, facts are the mind-independent truth-donors to which our beliefs must conform if they are to be true. But facts are not mind-independent and cannot be. For, as we know them, they are conceptually tainted. We can recognize as factual only those aspects of our experience which we have learned to interpret through the medium of our concepts. Facts, so to speak, are factitious; but if they are to be truth-donors, they must not be.

Although I am not, at the moment, trying to defend the correspondence theory of truth, I am trying to state it clearly enough to see whether it is worth defending. And if we admit the full force of the argument that we have just considered, it is doubtful if the theory can even be stated. For contrary to one of the accepted presuppositions of our enquiry, truth and error would no longer consist in a relationship between something mental and symbolic on the one hand, and an independent feature of reality on the other. It would consist rather in some kind of a relationship between beliefs and conceptual constructs. But does the argument have quite this force?

In the first place, we may object that the admission that facts as we deal with them are conceptualized does not entail either that facts do not exist or even that we can know nothing about them. On the contrary, if there were no facts, they could not be known through the medium of our concepts. And, if they are

*There would be small differences due to differences in visual capacity. (For example, dogs cannot see colours.)

known through this medium, then they are *known* in this guise. And it is no use complaining that it would be much better to know facts as they are in themselves and not as moulded and processed by our cognitive apparatus. For a human being, to know something *is* just for him to use his cognitive machinery, whether native or acquired, to the best advantage. To make any other demand is simply to utter a disguised (and futile) wish that our mental powers were other than they are. No doubt there are many facts in the universe that we are forever incapable of knowing because we either do not have or are incapable of having the concepts that would make them available to us. This means that there are many truths that are forever beyond us—and no doubt there are, both for this reason and for others. But that some facts are beyond our cognitive range because we lack the conceptual apparatus to bring them within it does not entail that we are incapable of knowing facts.

What we have to do in the face of the idealist objection is to emphasize the difference between facts and our cognizance of them. That this distinction is important in this context can be seen in the following way. If *per impossibile* there were brute unconceptualized facts to which we all had access, we might be able to explain true beliefs but how could we ever account for false ones? For one of the most important and prevalent ways of falling into error is by putting aspects of our experience into the wrong conceptual pigeonholes. And we are prone to do this precisely because the fragments of our sensory experience come to us in varying degrees of conceptualization. Familiar features are so well integrated into our structure of ideas that we assimilate them automatically and unthinkingly to the appropriate concept, *recognize* them, as we say, as such and such: this is an apple, that is snow, this is bread—and so on. But some features may be so unfamiliar that they are classified only with difficulty or not at all. Waking up in a strange room or from an anaesthetic, we may momentarily fail to place features of our environment because they seem totally unfamiliar. Outside of experimental situations in a psychological laboratory or in delirium, this is perhaps as near as most of us get to experiencing brute facts. And unusual or ambiguous aspects of accustomed surroundings may cause us hesitation. Is the moving grey shape glimpsed in the periphery of my visual field a mouse or a blown feather or just a hallucination? Walking in the twilight in Africa, I used to hesitate over classifying a dimly seen shape as a snake or a piece of rope or a stick.

Affirmations, whether true or false, consist of classifying experiences under the label suggested by the face-value conceptual aura that the experience carries with it. Sometimes these hints are fragmentary and misleading; and then we are apt to make mistakes. Even when experiences come to us in developed conceptual dress, we may still make mistakes. (For example, in identifying a pearl as genuine or a red stone as a ruby or a painting as a Constable or even a wax apple as an apple.) These instances are taken from the restricted area of sensory cognition; but the same principles apply elsewhere. They illustrate the point that it is not true that infection by concepts invalidates facts from serving as donors of truth or falsity. On the contrary, unless facts carry concepts with them, in however shadowy a form, they could not be recognized at all for what they are, the sources of the truth values of our beliefs. And we would not then be in a position to make any affirmations, true or false.

8 | Relations between truth-bearers and facts

We are now in a position to consider the last of the three main questions basic to the correspondence theory in the rather naive form in which it is raised by commonsense and which we have agreed to accept for this preliminary survey. Having discussed truth-bearers and facts, we must ask how they are related. The answer given by the theory is, of course, that they are related by correspondence—the truth-bearer corresponds to the fact if the belief or statement is true. But this is quite unexplanatory until we have decided what sense is to be put on the term 'correspond'. It is not helpful to substitute approximate synonyms for 'correspond'; to say that beliefs (or other truth-bearers) accord with, fit in with, agree with, tally with or match facts is no more enlightening.

Nor is it useful to consider standard uses of the verb 'correspond' to see if they can be tailored to fit the problem we are considering. The tickets on sale at the box office for a performance of a play certainly correspond to the seats in the theatre. But this merely means that tickets and seats are in a one-to-one relationship with one and only one ticket for each seat. There is not obviously such a relationship between true statements and facts; and, if there were, it would throw no light on the nature of truth. The sense in which two things may be said to correspond, match, fit or accord with one another obviously depends on the nature of the things that are being related. The word means different things in different cases. Portraits correspond with their originals, maps with their terrain, the score of a sonata with a performance, the Greek text of the *Odyssey* with a translation, a structural formula in chemistry with the organization of the molecule—the list could be extended indefinitely without bringing much insight into the problem.

It was partly because the nature of a relation of correspondence can vary so much with the nature of the matching terms of the relation that we spent so much time in examining candidates for the office of truth vehicle. If we had a clear answer to the question: what is a truth-bearer? we would be in a better position to know what kind of correspondence we are looking for. We did see that there are two types of answer to that question. We can accept *beliefs* (in some suitably unambiguous sense of the term) as our truth-carriers or we can opt for some linguistic form (sentence, statement). The great advantage of the second type of answer is, as we saw, that language has a *structure* and that this offers some hope of matching the linguistic structure of the sentence (let us say) with the organization of the fact. The advantage offered by the first answer is that many beliefs are said to be true or false which are not framed in language so that confining our attention to linguistic truth-bearers will omit some standard cases of truth and falsity from our survey and so from our final analysis. It was seen also that it is debatable whether a linguistic truth-bearer which is neither backed by a belief nor affirmed by a believer can properly be said to have a truth value at all.

We saw too, in examining the second term of this supposed relation, that facts are of different types and come to us with two structural components. They are mind-independent and objective features of the world and derive their skeleton, so to speak, from this objective nature. But they must be known in some conceptual dress, however flimsy or fragmentary it may be. And both of these layers have some kind of organization which truth-bearers have somehow to catch and convey.

Let us pay attention first to the structural elements in both truth-vehicle and truth-donor. This seems to offer us some sort of key to the problem. May we not reasonably suppose that we can identify the outlines of these structures and match them with each other? A structure or organization is a system of elements linked to each other by relations. And if we have two structures S_1 and S_2, we can ask if the elements of S_1 are reflected in S_2 in a one-one relationship. And if two elements in S_1, E_j and E_k are related by R_m, we can look to see if in S_2 corresponding elements and relation E_j', E_k' and R_m' stand in an analogous association. For example, we can compare two maps of different scales or a map with its terrain in this way. So too if the cat is on the mat, we can compare the fact with the sentence:

50. The cat is on the mat

We note that the animal is represented by the phrase 'the cat', what it is sitting on by the phrase 'the mat' and the spatial relation of cat to mat by the preposition 'on'. We find that language, in this simple instance, is a model of reality and that the sentence is true in virtue of the accuracy of the copy.

There has been more than one attempt in the recent history of philosophy to elucidate the nature of truth in this way.[23] But it would be generally accepted by philosophers that these accounts look plausible only for very simple instances of fact-matching language. Even in these cases, the explanatory promise is specious. Facts are not all of the same type, as we have already noted. And even if it could be shown that particular facts (that is, individuals instantiating properties or sets of individuals linked by relations) could be adequately mirrored in language in this way and that truth consisted in the accuracy of the reflection, the explanation could hardly by extended to general facts, still less to negations.

It is tempting to look on general facts as if they were simply conjunctions of particular facts. For example, it is a fact that all diamonds have a refractive index of 2·4. This fact is conveyed (and supposedly mirrored) by the true sentence:

51. All diamonds have a refractive index of 2·4

Is not 51 simply a shorthand version of a conjunction of statements of the type:

52. Diamond 1 has a refractive index of 2·4
53. Diamond 2 has a refractive index of 2·4
    . . .
54. Diamond n has a refractive index of 2·4

where there are n instances of diamond in the universe? The objection to this suggestion is well known. To suppose that general or universal statements are just synoptic catalogues of particular statements is to overlook the fact that general statements refer to *open classes* of particulars, not to a closed list. To claim an equivalence between:

55. All Xs have property Q

and

56. X_1 has property Q *and* X_2 has property Q *and* . . . X_n has property Q

is to make a claim with a vitally important suppressed clause namely: *and* $X_1, X_2 . . . X_n$ are all the Xs that there are. But to add this clause to 56 is to make it more than just a catalogue of particular statements. Thus there is no reason to suppose that general facts are simply conjunctions of particular facts.

Further, negative statements present an even more intractable difficulty. It looked as though statements of the type of 50 would make model cases for the hypothesis that language copied the world and that good copies were true statements. But what are we to say of:

57. The cat is not on the mat

What element of the fact is to be associated with 'not'? We are back again with the difficulties that we met in talking about negative facts. There are two alternative lines of argument open to us here. We can continue to maintain that there are negative facts with all the consequent difficulties that the supposition involves. But then we must abandon the view that language mirrors facts. For however plausible it may seem to claim that 50 reflects the fact that the cat is on the mat, it is certainly not possible to hold that 57 mirrors the negative fact in the same sense. For the feature of the sentence that makes it negative (the word 'not' in this case) has no corresponding element in the fact. The second alternative is to claim that negative statements are really disguised affirmatives, so that to say:

58. X does not have predicate P_1

is really shorthand for:

59. X is capable of having one of the predicates $P_1, P_2 . . . P_n$ *and* does in fact have *either* P_2 *or* P_3 *or* . . . *or* P_n

Whether 59 is really an acceptable analysis of 58, I will leave the reader to decide. At least we can say that it does not explain a negative statement as a conjunction of simple affirmatives. For it introduces the modal concept 'capable' which can itself certainly not be analysed as a conjunction of affirmative statements. No copy theory of language has shown how to explain sentences containing modal terms like 'capable', 'possible', 'necessary' and so on as copies of the corresponding facts.

It seems then that even if we admit that a copy theory of language is satisfactory for simple cases of particular affirmative statements and, for these cases, forms a basis for the correspondence theory of truth, it cannot be extended to give an account of general or negative sentences. But can it give a completely satisfactory explanation even in the simplest cases? Language is a symbolic system which provides a form of representation for what interests us, for what we want to reflect on or communicate. An important part of that field of interest is the world of fact. Symbolic systems are sets of signs which are controlled and made workable by two different kinds of rules, semantic rules which determine which signs stand for what features of the world and syntactic rules which regulate the way in which these signs are put together to form sentences. The regularities of usage and reference which are the outcome of these rules of language are conventional and arbitrary in the sense that they are the outcome of human habits and choices. That this is so is evident from the variety of different natural languages spoken in the world. Their rules of syntax and semantics vary from one language to the next but each is a perfectly efficient medium of thought and communication.

Not all symbolic systems are arbitrary in this way. Contrast, for example, two systems of recording musical information—the standard staff notation and recording music by magnetic tape. The second translates patterns of sound to patterns of magnetized particles in accordance with the laws of physics. The principles on which the recording is made are in no way arbitrary. That is to say, they are a part of nature and cannot be affected or changed by human decisions. The staff notation on the other hand is arbitrary in this sense. It is a system devised by human intelligence and could be changed (as it has been throughout its history) to make it more efficient and convenient. It could, for example, be replaced by the tonic sol-fa notation if that were to be found more useful.

From these instances it can be seen that codes for recording and communicating information (of whatever kind) can be based on two different types of law, conventional man-made rules, on the one hand, and the natural regularities of the universe, on the other. In the case of natural languages, the conventional rules are more obviously at work, though contemporary linguists have suggested that features common to all languages may be controlled by brain mechanisms.[24] If this were so, part at least of the structure of languages would be based on nature rather than convention.

With these considerations in mind, we can return to the question: can language picture the world in even the simplest type of declarative sentence? A safe, though not at first sight very illuminating, answer to this question would be: language can picture facts but there is no unique way in which it can do so. A natural language is, among other things, a code for representing and storing information. The rules according to which it carries out this task are not known innately; they have to be learned. And this is so whether the rules of the code are conventional or natural. A chemist who reads the constitution of a gas in a spectrograph is reading a representation of a structure; he might have come to learn the same facts by studying the gas by chromatography. He would then be learning the same facts from a different language; but both languages would have been learned. Analogously, we could have the same facts conveyed to us in English or in German or in any other language but only in one that we had acquired.

Perhaps this comparison helps to bring out the point and the weakness of the analogy between a linguistic description of a fact and a picture of the fact. Although sophisticated forms of pictorial representation embody conventional elements, simple ones seem to be intuitively transparent. The higher animals will react innately to three-dimensional representations of features of the world that they find interesting. A dog's attention can be attracted by a model of another dog; but it would have to be trained to react to a two-dimensional portrait. Monkeys can be intrigued, without special training, by the pseudo-three-dimensional appearance of their reflection in a mirror. We do not know whether the cave artists of Lascaux had to explain to their audience that the buffalo and hunters which they drew were intended to represent buffalo and hunters; but presumably they did not. At least they did not have to explain their own intentions to themselves. Thus some pictures, the simplest, can convey their information without the audience having to learn the rules according to which the original is represented. What is called *iconic* representation, which replicates the observable features—or some of them—of the original, seems to be innately understood, even by some non-human animals. But languages, of course, do not represent their subject matter iconically. At the risk of labouring the obvious it is worth noting just why this is so.

In the first place, symbolic systems, whether natural or conventional, have to be learned. The exceptional case of icons is an anomaly in this respect. And for that reason, the metaphor that language 'pictures' facts is a misleading metaphor. Ideographic forms of writing, like American Indian picture writing or archaic Chinese, represent a transition between iconic representation and a purely conventional script. But even they have to be learned and interpreted. Secondly, there is an obvious reason why language is an inefficient medium for picturing facts. Whether language is written or spoken, it is a one-dimensional linear medium and consequently at a disadvantage in representing a three- or four-dimensional world. A sentence is a succession of sounds following one another in time or a succession of inscriptions succeeding each other along one spatial axis. I suggested earlier, in speaking of a possible interpretation of propositions as the deep structures of sentences, that the tree diagrams of generative grammar were useful, among other ways, in spreading out sentence structure into a second spatial dimension. And this, so to speak, enlarges the pictorial versatility of natural language.

There is a third limitation to the usefulness of the picture or copy metaphor. The concept system according to which we anatomize and classify our world is incorporated into our native language. The nouns, verbs, adjectives and prepositions of English seem the natural correlates of the things, actions, qualities and relations, respectively, of which the world seems to be made up. Indeed, old-fashioned school grammar encouraged this superstition by its doctrine of 'parts of speech'. The fact is that our native language provides us with a ready-made conceptual scheme which can bias the way in which we see the world. If indeed all natural languages were of the same pattern so that the differences between them were merely minor matters of vocabulary and grammatical inflection, we might be prepared to conjecture that the structure of language does in some way mirror the structure of reality. If, for example, all the languages of the world were of the Indo-European pattern familiar to us from Latin, Greek, and most of the modern languages of Europe, the conjecture would have some inductive support. Many philosophers, from Thomas Reid in the eighteenth century to Bertrand Russell in our own time have been prepared to back this surmise.[25] But influential scholars in the field of linguistics, particularly in the present century, have brought it into question.

In the present century, the study of languages of very different origin and structure from those of the Indo-European family (in particular the native languages of the Americas) has brought to light evidence suggesting a very close causal relationship between a man's native language and his conceptual interpretation of his environment. The great American linguist, Edward Sapir, wrote: 'The relation between language and experience is often misunderstood. Language is not merely a more or less systematic inventory of the various items of experience which seem relevant to the individual, as is so often naively assumed, but is also a self-contained creative symbolic organisation, which not only refers to experience largely acquired without its help but actually defines experience for us by reason of its formal completeness and because of our unconscious projection of its implicit expectations into the field of experience.'[26] Elsewhere he says: 'The fact of the matter is that the "real world" is to a large extent built up on the language habits of the group. . . . We see and hear and otherwise experience very largely as we do because the language habits of our community predispose certain choices of interpretation.' A pupil of Sapir, B. L. Whorf, developed these ideas to claim that even the culture of a society was in part determined by the language spoken by its members.[27] We are concerned here with the narrower claim that the conceptual structure that we impose upon our experience of the world is constrained and determined by our native language and that 'the pie of experience can be sliced in all sorts of ways, and language is the principal directive force in the back-ground.'[28]

The detailed discussion of the Sapir–Whorf hypothesis, as it is called, would need more space than we can give it here.[29] No doubt it is a very difficult conjecture to support in its strongest form. But if there is even a small nucleus of truth in it, it has important consequences for this enquiry. It adds further strength to the already well-established contention that facts in so far as they are knowable are never concept-free. And it offers a decisive piece of evidence against the conjecture that language is a picture, copy or model of the world in any sense that would make a naive correspondence theory of truth at all intelligible.

One way of showing this is to consider some of the concrete instances of conceptual mis-matching involved in translating quite straightforward factual sentences from English to one of the more exotic languages studied by Sapir, Whorf and others. (Note [30] gives one of Whorf's examples, offered here simply in illustration of the hypothesis and not as any sort of proof.) The main point of the Sapir–Whorf conjecture, in the restricted version relevant to our subject, may be summarized thus. In translation from English to many languages which are closely related to English in origin or, at least, in structure, the concepts encoded in the sentence are mirrored by analogous concepts expressed in the other language. But in languages of very different structure, a close translation of the English sentence may encode quite different concepts. And this offers evidence against two closely associated assumptions basic to a correspondence view of truth: first, that facts, independent of us, are nevertheless known to us as they objectively are; secondly that language has some kind of structural similarity to the facts it purports to record. It is a difficult, controversial and so far unresolved problem to decide what weight to place on evidence of this kind. It is at least an indication of the close relevance of linguistics to philosophy.

The Sapir–Whorf hypothesis is not easy to state in a form that makes it open to decisive empirical tests. It is mentioned here only for the limited purpose of illustrating one way in which different symbolic media may present the same facts in very different conceptual guises. I do not, of course, mean to suggest that there is no common factual basis that underlies all our different ways of looking at the world. Progress in science replacing false scientific theories by closer approximations to reality is decisive evidence to the contrary. Some ways of conceptualizing the world are *truer* than others. So we must not deny that, in some way still to be made clear, concepts can be true of facts even though facts, *as we come to know them,* are known in a conceptual dress. This is an apparent paradox but one which any satisfactory account of truth must resolve.

For these reasons, among others, we cannot say that language copies or pictures facts. And perhaps this is just as well. For if the picture theory of meaning was correct, the information conveyed in language would be much poorer than it is. General, negative and modal statements would be incommunicable and much of what we now know would remain unknown. One of the main incentives for adopting such an over-simple account of the working of language is that it offers an easy explanation of the nature of correspondence. That the relation of language to fact is much more subtle and complex than this makes the correspondence theory that much more difficult to explain and defend. However, although language does not picture facts, it can carry, store and convey all the information that a picture could carry and more.

Consider the following 'experiment'. We have a room with a table and a cupboard containing a number of objects—knives, forks, plates, a vase of flowers, let us say. We arrange these in a certain pattern on the table, take a colour photograph of the scene and then replace the objects in the cupboard. If we then ask someone to use the photograph to guide him in setting the table as it was before, he will find no difficulty in doing so. Now repeat the same procedure except that instead of taking a photograph, we write a careful description of the arrangement of objects. We remove the objects as before and ask another subject to set out the table in accordance with the written description. He too will find no difficulty in doing so. In other words, all the information carried by the picture has been carried by the verbal description. We can make the transition from fact to language and back to fact without any distortion of the information required for the transition. The truth of the description is guaranteed by the accuracy with which the facts described have been reinstated.

Evidence of this kind can be used to show that although language is not a copy or picture of facts it can perform the function of a picture, when required, as well as other tasks which no picture could do. The difference between the photograph and the description in the imagined 'experiment' is that the photograph is a direct copy of the facts while the description is a coded copy rather in the way that a picture sent by telephone or radio is a coded copy during the course of transmission, or a tape recording of a symphony is a coded copy of the music. But whereas in the case of the picture sent by radio or the tape recording, the rules of the code are the laws of physics, the information conveyed in language is coded according to the semantic and syntactic rules of the language concerned, together with these laws of brain physiology which control the workings of language. Thus if correspondence between language and fact is to be a defensible account of the nature of truth, or a defensible part of such an account, we have to look to semantics and syntax, that is to say, questions of *meaning* to give us a clue about the nature of truth.

At the start of this section, I said that there were two different types of problem about the relation of truth-bearers to facts. We have discussed one of these which arose from regarding truth-bearers as linguistic and trying to relate the structural properties of languages to those of facts. The other line of enquiry arises from taking beliefs as truth-bearers. This raises new problems because not all of our beliefs, and perhaps not even most of them, are framed in language. Yet we cannot avoid attributing truth or falsity to beliefs, whether or not they are made explicit in words. But we do also attribute truth and falsity to the linguistic expressions in which our beliefs are expressed. Are we using the words 'true' and 'false' in the same sense in both these cases? If we are not, what are these different senses and how are they related? Is one of them derivative from the other?

These questions are not easy to answer. We have agreed that in so far as truth can be attributed to units of language, to statements and sentences, it is essentially bound up with the rules by which information about facts is coded into language. That is to say, an explanation of the nature of truth and error depends, as a necessary condition, on an explanation of the meaning rules of a language. Yet this cannot be the full story for several reasons. In the first place, meaning can be transmitted with fair accuracy[31] from one language to another. Suppose that we adapted the table-arranging 'experiment' outlined above by translating the English description of the arrangement on the table into German and then asked a German to re-set the table according to the verbal instructions in his own language. The final state of the table would match the original state, given an accurate translation. But the rules which relate the vocabulary to the world and the words to each other in English are quite different from the analogous rules in German. If this were not so, the languages would be identical. Thus though the semantic and syntactical rules of a language may be necessary for an explication of the notion of truth, they are certainly not sufficient.

We can explain the nature of this necessary condition a little more clearly by making a distinction between a form of words being *true of* a certain state of affairs and being a true statement. Suppose that here and now I describe an imaginary state of affairs and express it in a sentence as follows:

60. There is now a male moth of the species *Abraxas grossu-lariata* on the topmost spray of the currant bush on the west side of my garden

I do not affirm this sentence but merely entertain it as a possible state of affairs. Let us suppose further that there actually is a moth of that species in the spot described at the moment I am writing the words of 60. Would we say that 60 is true? Surely all that we would say, in the circumstances described, would be that 60 is *true of* the facts but that it would not be a true statement. To be true of a state of affairs is to be a linguistically adequate identification of the state of affairs described. A random sentence typed by a computer might well be true of something but we would properly hesitate to call it true *simpliciter*.

This suggests a second necessary condition for the truth of a sentence. For a sentence to be true it must not only be true of (that is, descriptively adequate to) a certain state of affairs but it must also be affirmed of that state of affairs. Descriptive adequacy is a weak form of truth applicable to sentences. The notion goes some way to resolve the dispute between those philosophers like Professor Hamlyn who deny that unasserted sentences are true or false and those who agree with Professor Geach (see pages 35 and 41 above). We can now say that Geach was right if by 'true' we mean 'weakly true', or 'descriptively adequate'. But if we intend the word in its strong sense, Hamlyn is right. For assertion does seem to be a necessary condition of truth in the strong sense (and, of course, of falsity as well).

But how is this related to the matter of true and false beliefs? There can be no question of asking that a *belief* shall, in general, be descriptively adequate or true of some state of affairs. For many human beliefs and all those of infants and animals are unformulated in any symbolic medium. Nor can such inarticulate beliefs be said to be asserted. For we can assert something only when it is expressed in language of some kind. Thus neither of the necessary conditions that we have proposed for the truth or falsity of sentences seem to apply to beliefs unless the belief has been clothed in words.

Some unformulated beliefs can indeed be *evinced in action*. When I put my key into the front door, I evince my belief that the key will open the door. When a dog digs in the garden, he may evince his belief that his bone is buried there. It might perhaps be suggested that evincing beliefs in action is the behavioural analogue of affirmation. But this analogy is unconvincing. Only a very small proportion, even of empirical beliefs, can be evinced in action. We cannot indicate by our behaviour that we hold a belief about the past or the future except in so far as there are present states of the world which show traces of the past or presage the future. For more remote events, we have to put our beliefs into language. I can evince my belief that it is going to rain by wearing a raincoat or carrying an umbrella. But I can express my belief in the heat death of the universe only in language.

It has sometimes been suggested that 'I believe P' can be explained as 'I have a tendency to act as if P were true'. But such an analysis must fail here for several reasons. In the first place, it makes use of the concept *true* which is itself the object of our enquiry. Secondly, we agreed earlier when talking about the ambiguity of 'belief' that in so far as belief is relevant to truth values, the word must be taken in the occurrent rather than the dispositional sense and must refer to the content rather than the act of believing. And tendencies are dispositions. Thirdly, it can easily be shown that if we accepted an equivalence between 'I believe P' and 'I have a tendency to act as if P were true' it would be impossible to say, without a vicious regress:

61. I have a tendency to act as if I believed P

And it is easy to imagine circumstances in which 61 would be a true statement.[32] Nor would it help to drop the reference to tendencies to believe and say instead that 'I believe P' is equivalent to 'I act as if P were true'. Apart from the objection already made, it is often true that someone does not believe a certain proposition and yet does act as if it were true (for example, in trying to mislead someone).

It is in fact extraordinarily difficult to offer a plausible analysis of belief which is not expressed in language without having to offer as well an account of truth which is inconsistent with any reasonable interpretation of the correspondence theory. We wish to equate 'belief' with 'content of a cognitive act'. But the belief with which we are concerned is unformulated in language. Let us consider some examples. Suppose that I believe that I have left my car key in the left-hand pocket of the jacket I was wearing yesterday. I might have a memory image of feeling the key in that pocket and an expectation of feeling it there again when I go to look. If I put my hand in the pocket and feel the key, it might be said that the truth of my belief consisted in the similarity of the tactile imagery of memory and expectation with the touch sensation which confirms my belief. This is as close as we can get to interpreting wordless belief as a correspondence between mental content and confirming fact. But this is a very special and unrepresentative case. In the first place, images are symbols. They stand for things absent from our experience and represent them to us. Thus beliefs that are mediated by imagery cannot rank as genuinely non-symbolic. Images are, of course, iconic signs which are replicas, however faded or distorted, of their originals; and they are natural signs, unlike words which are meaningful by convention. But they are symbolic, for all that. Secondly, images are an unrepresentative kind of symbol simply because people vary enormously in the degree to which they employ imagery in their thinking. Experimental studies by psychologists have established this point beyond doubt.[33] Some of us employ a great deal of imagery and some none at all. Thus there is no one type of non-verbalized belief that is expressed in images; and, in consequence, there is no one type of belief whose truth can be interpreted as consisting in a similarity between image and experience. If a particular belief of mine can be regarded in this way, it is a purely fortuitous result of the personal idio-syncrasies of my way of thinking. And so it cannot be used as a basis for an analysis of non-verbalized belief, or even of one special case of such belief. Nor is there, in the case of beliefs accompanied by imagery, any structure or stability in the imagery that would allow us even to hope to match image-structure with fact-structure as seemed plausible with beliefs expressed in language.

In any event, whatever might be claimed for particular beliefs, positive or negative, general beliefs could not possibly be expressed in any combination of images. For images at best are merely shadowy and fragmentary re-instatements of particular experiences; and they could, at most, be an ancillary symbolic aid to expressing a general belief. But might not an image stand for a class of experiences in the way in which a nominalist account of language makes a general word like 'dog' stand indifferently for any member of the class of dogs? Such an account of the working of general words is not easy to work out in detail but let us now allow, for the sake of the argument, that such a programme can be carried out. We would still have to ask what sense we can put on the word 'correspondence' in cases where this relation is supposed to hold between images and general beliefs. It is plain that in such cases we cannot say that the relation is one of similarity between image and percept, as was the answer in the case of particular beliefs. So even if we concede as much as can be conceded to such an account, there will still be many beliefs which are not expressed in language and which cannot be explained on these lines. And this is enough to leave us with our problem.

The content of the occurrence of a wordless belief must somehow represent to us the fact, real or putative, with which the belief is concerned. But how is it to do this without language or imagery or some other symbolic medium of representation? It is helpful to notice here that the principal point of difference between such bare beliefs and those expressed in language is that the former are, of necessity, much simpler. We saw earlier that to express a belief in words is to make it more precise, more detailed and more stable. But it can do much more. There are many beliefs which could not be entertained unless they were expressed in language (including extensions of natural language such as the symbolism of mathematics). It is obvious enough that a mathematician's belief in the general theory of relativity could not exist unless it was framed and sustained in an elaborate and specialized language. The same applies to most propositions other than those which reflect our immediate and particular concerns. It is the content-bearing capacity of beliefs that is so immensely extended by language. Without language, we would be restricted to particular beliefs about the here and now. Generalizations would be beyond us except in so far as the present particular could be dimly felt as somehow representative of others. Beliefs about the past and future would be available only in immediate expectations and short-term memories. The character of the more distant past and future would be beyond our grasp. Negations could only be appreciated as the vague awareness of the absence of something, felt as a relief or as a disappointment. We should, in other words, be in the state of mind of infants or animals, with our range of believing drastically curtailed by our poverty of expression.

What does the *content* of such beliefs consist in? We find this hard to answer because, having language available, we tend to verbalize any belief whose content is opaque or confused. So far as we can answer the question, such contents appear to be simply a certain 'set', as the psychologists call a directedness of attention and expectation. We are often made aware of these beliefs only when we are surprised or disappointed when experience fails to bear them out. But they must not be despised or neglected, for all that. Our most complex and sophisticated belief systems grow out of and are based on the primitive goal-seeking behaviour with which all animals, including the human animal, begin. The tendency to distinguish true from false is a self-perpetuating feature of animal behaviour. It is an essential factor in natural selection in that only those animals whose primitive beliefs are true on the whole tend to survive in a hostile environment. And it provides the continuous reinforcement which is necessary for the cognitive development of the individual and the species. Successful beliefs not only give the animal the opportunity of trying again in unfriendly surroundings; they encourage it to do so.

We must recognize however that these beliefs lack identifiable content; and for this reason, there is no sense in which they can be said to *correspond to* the facts to which they are directed. They are more like successful or unsuccessful adjustments to the environment whose truth or falsity lie simply in the success or failure of the adjustment. Such beliefs are in fact the model examples for the pragmatic theory of truth which tries to equate what is true with what is useful in practice. And it is the principal failing of the pragmatic theory that it is plausible only for such primitive and unrepresentative beliefs. But as a theory of truth for infants and animals, it meets the facts very well. However, as human beings, we are principally interested in that vast range of beliefs which are expressed in language. For these, the correspondence theory is still, for all its difficulties, a more promising prospect.

9 | Résumé

So far we have been looking at the correspondence theory from a commonsense viewpoint and trying to see what it could mean to say that truth consisted in correspondence with fact. This has required us to look at different senses in which the word 'true' can be used, at possible candidates for the office of truth-bearer, at the nature of facts and the relation between truth-bearers and facts. Little of what has been said up to now has been conclusive and we have made rather free use of the notion of a *concept* without explaining precisely how the term is to be taken. But the purpose of the discussion so far has simply been to identify some points of difficulty and to make a foundation and framework for later argument.

One effect of this discussion has been to raise legitimate doubts about the propriety of the phrase 'the correspondence theory of truth'. In the two following chapters, we shall be looking at theories which have tried to make explicit what might be referred to by this phrase; and we shall see that there are good reasons for doubting whether they succeed.

In the meantime, we have distinguished a number of senses in which the word 'true' may occur. And even at the elementary level at which the discussion has proceeded, it can be seen that some of these senses are irrelevant to the concept of correspondence and that others of them raise very wide-ranging and difficult problems in the theory of knowledge which go well beyond the confines of the traditional correspondence theory. In particular:

(a) Truth of expression consists in the linguistic correctness of a statement as an expression of a speaker's belief. This is a matter of conformity with the semantic conventions which govern the use of the words and phrases of a given language, a question, in other words, for semantics or the theory of meaning. It is a *necessary* condition for a given utterance to be true in the strongest sense of the word; but other conditions are necessary as well.

(b) Truth of cognition is a much more complex matter. A belief purports to be a representative conceptualized extract of the objective world of independent fact. (We have already said something about 'facts' and there will be more to be said in Part II.) The process of extraction consists in the working of all those cognitive functions that are the material for the theory of knowledge and the psychology of cognition—sensation, perception, concept formation, judgement and the rest. At this point, the phrase 'correspondence theory of truth' is seen to be a piece of uninformative shorthand for answers to the main problems of epistemology and cognitive psychology.

(c) A truth-bearer is *weakly true* if it is a descriptively adequate expression that is not actually affirmed of the situation which it adequately describes. The full analysis of this concept will clearly depend on the answers that we give at (a) and (b) above. That is to say, the analysis must wait on a satisfactory semantics and an adequate theory of knowledge.

(d) A truth-bearer is *strongly true* if it is weakly true and also is used to refer to the situation that it adequately describes. This raises the question of what we mean by 'affirmation' or 'assertion'. Something has already been said on this point but it will be discussed further in the final chapter with particular reference to the question: in what sense, if any, is assertion relevant to truth as correspondence?

(e) We have noted (on page 78) that there is a sense of the word 'true' in which *concepts* can be said to be *true of* the facts. This is a new sense of 'true' which is a predicate normally restricted to the truth-bearers that we have discussed—sentences, statements and the rest. But clearly there is a sense in which concepts like *dog, oxygen, electron* are true of reality in which concepts like *witchcraft, unicorn* or *phlogiston* are not. This again is a problem of the theory of knowledge which lies beyond our immediate concern but of which any complete theory of truth would have to take account.

Part II

1 | The semantic theory of truth

What has been said in the previous chapters will have been enough to show that the commonsense idea of empirical truth as consisting in a correspondence between truth-bearers and the facts to which they relate becomes very confused on closer examination. Neither the nature of facts nor of truth-bearers is obvious; and in consequence, the relation between them cannot easily be explained. Having arrived at this unsatisfactory position as a result of trying to make our pre-analytic concept of truth precise and explicit, it may now be useful to examine the problem from the other side. Let us look at an established theory of truth which is clear, precise and systematic and ask how far it stands up to criticism. There is one very famous version of the correspondence theory which satisfies this description—Tarski's semantic theory of truth.

This theory was first set out by Tarski in a long and very technical paper in 1931[34] and explained in a more popular and readable version in 1944.[35] However the second paper gives a very cursory account of the technical concept of *satisfaction* which is basic to the semantic theory. It cannot therefore be fully understood on its own. In what follows, I shall try to explain the theory in as untechnical a form as is consistent with providing a fair basis for criticism. This is not easy as the semantic theory is hard to understand.

Tarski starts his account by laying down the conditions that a satisfactory definition of the notion of truth must meet. It must be both 'materially adequate' and 'formally correct'. By the material adequacy of his definition he means that 'it aims to catch hold of the actual meaning of an old notion' and does not purport merely to stipulate that the familiar word 'truth' shall be used in a restricted technical sense as, for example, terms like 'force' and 'work' are used in physics. To avoid the difficulties connected with the variety of possible truth-bearers he restricts the application of the word to *sentences*. And to remove the type-token ambiguity which arises in connection with the term 'sentence'[36] he explains in a footnote that 'for our present purposes, it is somewhat more convenient to understand by "expressions", "sentences" etc., not individual inscriptions but classes of inscriptions of similar form (thus, not individual physical things but classes of such things)'.[37]

It is, however, a disadvantage of all definitions which claim to express the familiar everyday sense in which 'true' and 'truth' are applied to empirical statements that none of them is sufficiently clear and precise. Tarski considers Aristotle's well known definition, 'To say of what is that it is not, or of what is not that it is, is false, while to say of what is that it is, or of what is not, that it is not, is true', and says of it that it is more satisfactory in respect of clarity and precision than more modern formulations such as 'The truth of a sentence consists in its agreement with (or correspondence to) reality.' It is at any rate this traditional concept of truth that he wishes to present in a form which will satisfy the demands of contemporary logic.

He introduces the question of the material adequacy of his proposed definition in the following way. If we take a commonplace sentence expressing a familiar empirical truth such as

62. Snow is white

and ask under what conditions we accept this sentence as true, we can express the condition in the following equivalence:

63. The sentence 'snow is white' is true if and only if snow is white

In this unexceptionable, if unenlightening, statement, we have the sentence 'snow is white' occurring twice, first in quotation marks and then without them. This is because the first occurrence of the phrase in question is the name of the sentence and the second is the sentence itself. And it is an important convention of modern logic to distinguish between *using* a term and *mentioning* that term in just this way. The sentence itself says something about the world; but to say that the sentence is true is to say something about the sentence. We use the sentence in saying something about the world; we mention the sentence—and in mentioning it *we use its name*—in saying that it is true. (This convention is not a pointless formality but a safeguard against some subtle fallacies.)

Tarski goes on to generalize the procedure expressed in 63 by replacing an arbitrary sentence which is a candidate for a truth value by the letter p and replacing the name of this sentence by X.[38] If we then ask: what is the relation between the two sentence-forms 'X is true' and p? it is clear that the answer must be that they are equivalent and therefore, the following equivalence holds:

64. X is true if, and only if, p

If we replace p in 64 by any sentence and X by its name, we have what Tarski calls 'an equivalence of the form (T)'. And it will be a criterion of the material adequacy of his proposed definition if all equivalences of the form (T) follow from that definition. 64 is not itself a definition of truth nor are its substitution-instances, the equivalences of the form (T)—such as 63 above and the like. At best they can be considered 'partial definitions' of truth.

So far we have talked as if the concept of truth that Tarski is trying to make clear and specific is the one with which we are familiar in our own native languages. But at this point Tarski raises a difficulty. Any ordinary natural language can be shown to be capable of generating antinomies or contradictions. For example:

65. The sentence on this page which contains two tokens of the word 'false' is false

Clearly, 65 refers to itself and says of itself that it is false. But if it is in fact false, then what it says is not true. And if it is in fact false and says of itself that it is not true, it must really be true. But if it is taken to be true, it follows that it is false. Whichever truth value we assign to it, we are forced to conclude that it has the other. Thus since we have both:

66. If 65 is not true, then 65 is true

as well as:

67. If 65 is true, then 65 is not true

we may conclude, by standard rules of logic:

68. 65 is true, if and only if 65 is not true

Any language which generates a contradiction is unacceptable to a logician. Among other things, in an inconsistent language any statement can be shown to be provable. For this and other reasons, Tarski concludes that '*the problem of the definition of truth obtains a precise meaning and can be solved in a rigorous way only for those languages whose structure has been exactly specified*'.[39]

If we examine the assumptions that led to the contradiction expressed in 68, we find that there are two which are so obvious and naturally accepted that we do not ordinarily think of them as 'assumptions' at all. They are:

(a) that our language contains not only expressions but also the names of those expressions as well as terms like 'true' and 'false' which refer to sentences of the language.

(b) that the ordinary rules of logic apply to our language, in particular, that we assume that a sentence is either true or false.

It is indeed possible to reject (b) but only if we have at our disposal a developed logic of more than two truth values. This leads to complexities that lead far from the hoped-for simplicities of a correspondence theory of truth. But (a) may be rejected without (b). And this is, in fact, the course that Tarski takes. A language which has the properties listed in (a) Tarski calls a 'semantically closed' language; and to avoid the difficulties resulting from the structure of such languages, he decided not to use such a language in the formulation of his definition.

But if we are to avoid 'semantically closed' languages, certain rather elaborate precautions must be taken. In the first place, we must specify precisely what the structure of our language is to be. In the second place, we need another language in which to talk *about* the language whose structure we have specified and for which we are seeking a definition of truth. The first language is called the *object-language*; and the second language in which we talk about the object-language is known as the *meta-language*. If we are to be able to talk about our object-language in the meta-language, it will clearly be convenient if the meta-language contains the object-language as a part of itself. (There are technical devices for avoiding this inclusion of the one language within the other, but it is simpler not to have to resort to these.) In addition, the meta-language must contain *names* for all the sentences of the object-language as well as semantic terms like 'true' and 'false' along with the standard vocabulary of logic (containing such terms as 'if . . . then', 'if and only if' and so on). Tarski adds that it is desirable that semantic terms which refer to the object-language should be introduced into the meta-language by definition. 'For, if this postulate is satisfied, the definition of truth, or of any other semantic concept, will fulfil what we intuitively expect from every definition; that is, it will explain the meaning of the term being defined in terms whose meaning appears to be completely clear and unequivocal. And, moreover, we then have a kind of guarantee that the use of semantic concepts will not involve us in any contradictions.'[40]

Tarski's object-language (in his original paper) was the calculus of classes. This is a simple language with the following compo-nents.

Constants

There are four of these:
1. the negation sign: $-$
2. a sign for logical disjunction: v
3. the universal quantifier: (Ax) where 'x' is a variable
4. the inclusion sign: $\subset$ where '$x \subset y$' is to be read as 'x is included in y'. It is to be noted that one class is said to be included in another if every member of the first class is a member of the second. Thus we may say that a class is in-cluded in itself as a special case of this relation.

Variables

Variables stand for classes of individuals and will be written as the letter 'x' followed by a numerical subscript, thus: $x_1, x_2, x_3 \ldots x_n$. This will give us as many classes as we need. (In fact, Tarski requires an infinity of them.)

Well-formed formulas

These are constructed in accordance with the following rules:

R1: Any variable is a well-formed formula (*wff*, for short).
R2: Any two variables linked by the inclusion sign ($\subset$) is a *wff*. For example: '$x_1 \subset x_2$' is a *wff*.

R3: Any *wff* bracketed and preceded by the negation sign $(-)$ is a *wff*.

R4: Any *wff* preceded by the universal quantifier is a *wff*. For example: '$(Ax_2)-(x_1 \subset x_2)$' is a *wff*.

For our meta-language, we can use capital Xs (with subscripts) for variables and ordinary English for the constants. For example, the *wff* given as an example for R4 can be read, in the meta-language:

For all X_2, it is not the case that X_1 is included in X_2.

Tarski uses a special symbolism for part of his meta-language but for an untechnical explanation of his theory, this is not necessary.

The *wff*'s of the object language fall into two classes. If there is at least one variable in the formula that is not bound by a quantifier, the formula is a *sentential function* and is neither true nor false. If all the variables are bound, then the formula is a sentence and has a truth value. Examples of this are given below.

The calculus of classes is, of course, a part of formal logic which can be developed axiomatically and Tarski uses a version of the axioms of *Principia Mathematica* as the axiomatic basis of his system. He then gives rules for deriving theorems from his axioms. For the purposes of elucidating the concept of truth in his object-language, we need not examine these procedures which are a part of standard logic. One point, however, is worth a comment. If we have a formal system in which *wff*'s can be correctly derived from a true and consistent set of axioms, we seem to have in that very fact a guarantee that the provable sentences of the system will be true. Why then do we require a further explication of the notion of truth if all the provable sentences of the formal system are true? Tarski meets this point and explains that although all provable sentences of the system are true, it can be shown that there are true sentences which are *wff*'s of the system but are not themselves provable in it. 'Thus the definition of true sentence which we are seeking must also cover sentences which are not provable.'[41]

Tarski is now in a position to specify a convention to which true sentences of his object-language must conform. He calls this 'Convention T'.[42] This convention states that the definition of truth that he is seeking will be an *adequate definition* if it is formally correct and has as consequences the following:

(a) all sentences which are obtained from the expression 64 'X is true if and only if p' by substituting for X a name of a sentence of the object-language in question and for the symbol p the expression which forms the translation of this sentence into the meta-language;

(b) the sentence 'for any x, if x is a member of the class of true expressions, then x is a sentence'.

If the object-language contained only a finite number of sentences, we could, says Tarski, construct a correct definition of truth without difficulty simply by listing the true sentences as a disjunction of the form:

x is a true sentence if and only if it is either S_1 or S_2 or . . . or S_n

where there are only n true sentences in L and each of the S's is spelled out as an appropriate substitution instance of the form (T).

However, since there is no limit to the possible number of sentences true in L, we cannot use this method. Tarski therefore adopts a more roundabout route to his goal, and a very subtle and difficult one. The basic concept that he employs in formulating his definition of truth is the concept of *satisfaction*. Satisfaction is a relation between objects and well-formed formulas of L. We have seen that some of these formulas are sentential functions, that is to say, expressions of L which are neither true nor false because they contain one or more unbound variables. For example:

69. x is white
70. y is larger than z

are sentential functions (or open sentences). They can be transformed into sentences (and therefore into expressions with truth values) in either of two ways. (a) We can replace the variables with individual names, thus:

71. Snow is white
72. London is larger than Dublin

Or (b) we can bind the variables with quantifiers, thus:

73. (For every x) x is white
74. (There is an x and a y such that) x is larger than y

We could then assign truth values to the resulting sentences as follows: 71, 72 and 74 are true and 73 is false.

D

Let us confine our attention for the moment to open sentences. We have in school algebra open sentences (called 'simple equations') of the type:

$$x - 3 = 7$$

And we say that there is a unique number (in this case 10), which *satisfies* the equation. With a slightly more complex type of equation, say:

$$x^2 + 3x - 4 = 0$$

we need two numbers to satisfy the equation (in this case, -4 and $+1$).

Tarski extends this concept to open sentences of the object-language: 'For every a, we have a satisfies the sentential function "x is white" if and only if a is white (and from this we conclude, in particular, that snow satisfies the function "x is white").'[43] And for expressions with two free variables we proceed in the same way: 'for all a and b, a and b satisfy the sentential function "x sees y" if and only if a sees b.'[44] Thus if John sees the Eiffel Tower, John and the Eiffel Tower (in that order) satisfy the open sentence 'x sees y'.

However since we cannot set any limit to the number of free variables that may occur in a sentential function, Tarski decides not to talk of objects satisfying a given function but says rather that 'a given infinite sequence of objects satisfies a given sentential function'.[45] If our language L is that of the calculus of classes, we can number each of the classes and number correspondingly the free variables of the sentential function. We can then say that the infinite sequence f of classes satisfies the sentential function 'X_m is included in X_n' if and only if the class X_m (that is to say, the mth member of the infinite sequence of classes f) is included in the nth member of the sequence, x_n.

When the sentential function contains a universal quantifier, as for example:

$$(Ax_2)\ (x_1 \subset x_2)$$

a sequence of classes f will be said to satisfy the function if the following two conditions are fulfilled:

(a) the sequence f satisfies the function 'X_1 is included in X_2'
(b) the sequence does not cease to satisfy it even if the second

term of the sequence varies in any way at all. In other words, whatever class may appear as the second term of the infinite sequence of classes, the sequence still satisfies the function.

The requirements for satisfaction may be summarized in the following definition:

The sequence f satisfies the sentential function X if and only if f is an infinite sequence of classes and X is a sentential function and they fulfil one of the following four conditions:

  (a) there exist natural numbers m and n such that $X = x_m \subset x_n$ and the mth term of f is included in the nth term of f;
  (b) there is a sentential function Y such that $X = $ not–Y and f does not satisfy the function Y;
  (c) there are sentential functions Y and Z such that $X = $ Y or Z and f satisfies either Y or Z.
  (d) there is a natural number k and a sentential function Y such that $X = (Ax_k)Y$ and every infinite sequence of classes which differs from f in at most* the kth place satisfies Y.

Let us consider a simple example to exemplify condition (d). If a sentential function has a universal quantifier, the class variable bound by the quantifier, (supposing that it is the kth) ranges over every class in any infinite sequence of classes that occupies the kth place in the sequence.

Suppose now that we have an expression with more than one quantifier, say:

$$(Ax_m)\ (Ax_n)\ (x_m \subset x_n)$$

This is an expression with no unbound variables and so is a sentence. We proceed as follows. First, take the unquantified expression:

$$(x_m \subset x_n)$$

This is satisfied by any infinite sequence f whose mth term is included in its nth. If we now add one quantifier, we get:

$$(Ax_m)\ (x_m \subset x_n)$$

This expression, (which is still a sentential function since it has one unbound variable) will be satisfied by f and by any sequence

*'At most' is ambiguous. Here it means 'only if at all'.

differing from f at most in its mth term. That is to say, the un-quantified function is still satisfied if we replace the sequence f by any other sequence which differs from f only in having a different mth term. If this were so, *any* class would be included in the class forming the nth term of f. (Clearly, this would be the case only if the nth term of f were the universe class.)

Lastly, we add the second quantifier, obtaining:

$$(Ax_m)\ (Ax_n)\ (x_m \subset x_n)$$

This will be satisfied by the sequence f only if f satisfies (Ax_m) $(x_m \subset x_n)$ and, in addition, still satisfies it if, in accordance with (d) of the definition above, when the nth term of the sequence is replaced by any class whatever. This will mean that the sentence would be satisfied if and only if every class were included in every other class, which is clearly not the case.

Thus no sequence satisfies this sentence. Consider, now, for comparison the sentence:

$$(Ax_n)\ (x_n \subset x_n)$$

It is obvious that the unquantified expression:

$$(x_n \subset x_n)$$

is satisfied by any sequence whatever (and so by f whatever f may be), since every class is included in itself. And if we add the quantifier, we add the requirement that the expression will still be satisfied if f is replaced by a sequence which differs from it (if at all) only in its nth term. And clearly, in view of the fact that every class is included in itself, this will also be the case.

Tarski comes accordingly to his definition of truth:

S is a true sentence if and only if it is satisfied by every infinite sequence of classes.[46]

Correspondingly, a sentence S is false if and only if it is satisfied by no sequence at all. Tarski accepts this definition as satisfactory since it meets the conditions for such a definition which he laid down at the start of his enquiry: (i) it is formally correct in that there is no flaw in his logic and (ii) it is materially adequate in that it meets the conditions laid down in his Convention T. (See page 93 above.) He does not attempt a formal proof that the definition meets the requirements of his convention as this proof would demand a new formal apparatus. He does however show by a number of concrete examples that his definition has the properties that he requires of it.

There is no doubt whatever that the semantic theory of truth is a distinguished achievement of formal semantics. But the question that we have to consider is whether it can be used to lend any precision to the commonsense pre-analytic notion of empirical truth with which the correspondence theory has traditionally been concerned. And when we start to consider this question we are met by a curious difference of opinion among philosophers. There are at least three schools of thought on this topic.

In the first section of his classical paper[47] Tarski concludes a survey of the difficulties of a definition of truth by admitting that 'the very possibility of a consistent use of the expression "true sentence" which is in harmony with the laws of logic and the spirit of everyday language seems to be very questionable'. And having said this, he goes on to restrict himself to formalized languages with the results that we have just considered. Some years later, in what he calls the 'polemical' second part of his more popular paper, he wrote: 'I hope nothing which is said here will be interpreted as a claim that the semantic conception of truth is the "right" or indeed the "only possible" one. . . . I must confess that I do not understand what is at stake in such disputes: for the problem is so vague that no definite solution is possible.'[48] He explains that all he has tried to do is to clarify one of a group of associated concepts, none of which had so far been put in 'an intelligible and unequivocal form'. He does however believe that his formulation 'does conform to the intuitive content of that of Aristotle' (see page 92 above). 'I clearly realise' he went on, 'that the common meaning of the word "*true*"—as that of any other word of everyday language— is to some extent vague and that its usage more or less fluctuates. . . . In spite of all this, I happen to believe that the semantic conception does conform to a very considerable extent with the common-sense usage, though I readily admit I may be mistaken.' Thus Tarski's position seems to be that an adequate treatment of this question can only be undertaken by formal methods and that the concept of empirical truth can only be relativized to a particular language and to a formalized language at that. Nevertheless, when this has been done, we will have come as near as possible to putting the everyday concept of empirical truth into a precise and unequivocal form.

A second attitude to this question can be found in the writings of a group of philosophers who accept the work of Tarski as a foundation but believe more strongly than he does that the semantic theory of truth can be used to further an account of truth applicable to natural languages. It would be misleading to suggest that Professors Karl Popper, Donald Davidson and Richard Montague have much more in common than an acceptance of Tarski's work as a secure basis for their own. But each of them has used the semantic theory in interesting new ways.[49] Montague has argued, for example, that there is no important difference between formal and natural languages. Rather there is sufficient of a formal structure to English or to any other natural language to make it possible to apply formal theories of semantics to them. Davidson has offered a version of the correspondence theory of truth analogous to Tarski's except that it applies to natural languages and makes truth a property not simply of a sentence but rather of a sentence used on a particular occasion by a particular speaker. Popper has used Tarski's theory of truth to develop his own concept of 'verisimilitude', a key notion in his realist theory of knowledge. I shall not have space to discuss these developments here but I mention them to show that Tarski's theory is currently influential in philosophy and that not all philosophers agree with him in limiting its currency to formalized languages.

But there is a third group of philosophers who, though they admit the formal correctness of Tarski's treatment of the problem, nevertheless doubt its relevance to the traditional problem of truth. Among these are Professor Max Black, Professor P. F. Strawson and, recently, Mr J. L. Mackie.[50] We shall be considering Strawson's views on truth in the next chapter and it will be sufficient here to note his attitude to the semantic theory. Roughly speaking, his objection is that the semantic theory treats 'true' as a property of sentences when in fact it is not a property of anything because it is not a property at all. Further, it misuses the phrase 'true if and only if' by making it a synonym for 'means that' and so confuses the concept of meaning and truth. These are serious objections but we may defer consideration of them until we look at Strawson's own views on truth.

In the meantime, we may note that there is no consensus among competent critics about the bearing of Tarski's theory on the traditional realist account of truth as consisting in a correspondence between truth-bearers and facts. Let us now look at some objections which can be brought against the theory.

A great many objections have been made to the semantic theory of truth. In his book, *Das Wahrheitsproblem und die Idee der Semantik*, Professor Wolfgang Stegmüller lists no fewer than a dozen lines of criticism of Tarski's theory. Stegmüller himself is a strong proponent of the semantic point of view and he sets out the objections in order to refute them. But none of the objections are trivial and a good deal could be made of some of them by a determined critic. However I shall be concerned chiefly with other lines of criticism of the semantic theory which have not so far been much discussed.

(a) The first point concerns the importance that Tarski attaches to the distinction between object-language and meta-language and to the formal character of the object-language. Tarski attaches great importance to the fact that natural languages, being 'semantically closed' can generate paradoxes like that of the self-referring sentence on page 93. But why should a philosopher worry over this if he is concerned with the problem of truth in *natural* languages? The fact that a formal language contains a hidden source of contradiction is a serious and disabling flaw. For it can be shown that if there is a contradiction in a formal system, any proposition at all can be proved in the system. And a formal system in which anything can be proved is clearly useless. For this and other reasons, it is of cardinal importance to ensure that a formal language is free from contradiction. But a natural language which has no clearly formulated rules to determine what is and is not a well-formed formula of the language and no precise rules of inference other than those of pre-analytic conventional reasoning is under no necessity of avoiding contradiction at all costs. In a natural language, paradoxes and contradictions are no more than interesting curios; in a formal language they are a lethal defect.

Thus the philosopher interested in the problem of truth in natural languages does not have to take the elaborate antiseptic precautions that Tarski and all logicians must take in constructing their formal systems. Providing that he takes note of the distinction between using words and mentioning them where neglect of this distinction is likely to lead to confusion, he can even omit to mark out formally the boundary between object-language and meta-language.

If this is so, the natural language philosopher can object to the formalist that the logical precautions necessary in the construction and use of formal languages bring with them the serious disadvantage that the definition of truth that can be offered is simply a definition of 'true-in-L' where L is the formalized language in question. Tarski would, of course, concede this. For him, this restriction is part of the price we pay for a clear and accurate definition of truth. But it is a good reason for doubting his belief that 'the semantic conception does conform to a very considerable extent with the commonsense usage'.[51]

We do not seem to have any use in ordinary discourse for phrases like 'true in English', 'false in German' and the like. If someone was to say 'It is true in French that *chou* means "cabbage",' this would be taken to be a slightly eccentric and barely grammatical way of saying 'It is true *that in French chou* means "cabbage".' But however this may be, the basic reason for rejecting the concept of truth as relative to the language in which the true sentence is expressed is this: we want to insist that the fact that a given sentence S is true in one language is of itself a sufficient reason for claiming that a correct translation of S into any other language will also be true. Once the truth value of a sentence is assigned, any translation or paraphrase which preserves its cognitive content must also preserve its truth value. Truth in natural languages is an intensional and not an extensional concept. Exactly what this involves will be clearer when we have looked more critically at the notion of satisfaction.

(b) A second source of doubt about the semantic theory arises from Tarski's truth-bearers. At this point the precision and formality of the semantic theory masks an underlying vagueness.

We have seen earlier that there is an important distinction between a token-sentence and a type-sentence. The first is the individual physical utterance or inscription and the second is what the tokens have in common in virtue of which they are spoken of as tokens of the same type. This common content is again ambiguous. It might be taken to refer to the similar physical sound structure of the utterance or physical conformation of the inscription; or it might more plausibly be understood to refer to the meaning-load (or cognitive content) of the sentence. Tarski does not make it clear what 'sentence', in his usage, refers to. As we have seen, a footnote in his second paper says that 'for our present purposes it is somewhat more convenient to understand by "expressions", "sentences" etc., not individual inscriptions but classes of inscriptions of similar form'. But elsewhere he seems to take a different view. In a recent popular paper he wrote: 'Sentences are treated here as linguistic objects, as certain strings of sounds or written signs.'[52]

Let us assume that Tarski does mean 'sentence-type' when he says 'sentence'. There are two different ways of constructing types out of tokens. We may say that the type is what the tokens have in common. (This might be called the intensional view.) Or we can say, as Tarski does, that he is referring to *classes* of inscriptions of similar form. This is the extensional view, characteristic of formal logicians who find it easier to manipulate classes than meanings. Suppose now that we ask further: what is the property in virtue of which sentences $s_1, s_2, \ldots s_n$ are all held to be tokens of the sentence-type S? Is it the common meaning-load of the sentences or is it their similar physical qualities? Tarski would accept the second of these alternatives. 'Every deductive discipline is a system of sentences, which we shall also call *meaningful sentences*. The sentences are most conveniently regarded as inscriptions, and thus as concrete physical bodies. Naturally, not every inscription is a meaningful sentence of a given discipline: only inscriptions of a well-determined structure are regarded as meaningful.' 'And' he adds in a footnote, 'Instead of "meaningful sentence" we could say "well-formed sentence".'[53] In other words, the meaning of sentences for Tarski is not a matter of their *content* but rather of their *structure*. A sentence is meaningful if it has a place in a formal system in virtue of the fact that it has been constructed in accordance with the formation rules of the system. Thus, a sentence with meaning is a well-formed formula and not an *interpreted* expression. That is, it does not have to be assigned a descriptive content in order to have a meaning. Thus expressions such as 'F*a*', '(x) (F*x*⊃G*x*)' are meaningful whether or not they are given interpretations like 'John is tall', 'All men are mortal' and so on. The point is made clearly by Tarski in a recent popular paper: 'The syntactical rules should be purely formal, that is, they should refer exclusively to the form (the shape) of expressions; the function and the meaning of an expression should depend exclusively on its form.'[54] It is important to bear these statements in mind when we try to find out exactly what Tarski means by 'satisfaction'. We have to remember that in everyday parlance, a sentence is true or false partly in virtue of its cognitive content, that is, its ordinary descriptive meaning. Can the concept of satisfaction provide a substitute for this?

(c) The notion of satisfaction and the use to which Tarski puts it are crucial to the semantic theory. Here it is important to bear in mind that the concept is introduced in application to *sentential functions*, that is, to expressions which are not sentences because they contain unbound variables and in consequence do not have truth values. For example:

> x is white
> y is larger than z
> x is between y and z

are sentential functions with one, two and three unbound variables respectively.

The concept is introduced as a relation between objects and sentential functions or open sentences. The 'object' may be classes of individuals as in Tarski's exposition considered above or individuals of various types. Let us look first at the words in which Tarski introduces the concept:

The simplest and clearest case is that in which the given sentential function contains only *one* free variable. We can then significantly say of every single object that it does or does not satisfy the given function. In order to explain the sense of this phrase we consider the following scheme:

for all a, a satisfies the sentential function x if and only if p

and substitute in this scheme for '*p*' the given sentential function (after first replacing the free variable occurring in it by '*a*' and for '*x*' some individual name of this function. Within colloquial language we can in this way obtain, for example, the following formulation:

for every a, we have a satisfies the sentential function 'x is white' if and only if a is white

(and from this conclude, in particular, that snow is white).[55]

Or this, from Professor Quine: 'The open sentence '*x* walks' is satisfied by each walker and nothing else. The open sentence '*x*>*y*' is satisfied by each descending pair of numbers and no other pairs.'[56]

To explanations of this kind, we are naturally tempted to ask how we know that, for example, snow satisfies '*x* is white' without already knowing that the sentence 'snow is white' is true. How do we know that blood or soot do *not* satisfy '*x* is white' without knowing that the sentences 'Blood is white' or 'soot is white' are false? Indeed it is obvious that we cannot identify the individuals that satisfy an open sentence without knowing the truth value of the closed sentences resulting from substituting in it the names of the individuals for the unbound variable. That being so, is not an explanation of truth and falsity in terms of satisfaction plainly circular?

To this objection, a defender of the semantic theory of truth will reply that the theory is designed simply to give a clear and precise *definition* of truth. It does not pretend to offer a method of determining which particular sentences are true and which are false. The reply is justified but it does point to a feature of the theory that seriously limits its philosophical interest. It might be thought to be a strange kind of definition which was no aid to identifying members of the class defined.

(d) An essential move in the construction of the semantic theory is the move from the open sentence which has no truth value to the closed sentence which does. But since the concept of satisfaction is crucial to the theory, Tarski has to find a means of applying this notion to closed sentences after he has defined and demonstrated it for open sentences. Unless he does this, he cannot arrive at his definition of true sentence as a sentence which is satisfied by all sequences. Stegmüller, in his book on formal semantics, described the move by which Tarski makes the transition from sentential function to sentence as an artifice (*Kungstgriff*) and even as a trick (*Trick*). But these descriptions are not pejorative. Stegmüller does not suggest that the device is in any way illegitimate; he is merely drawing attention to an ingenious piece of logical sleight of hand.

An open sentence with two unbound variables may be satisfied by sequences of ordered pairs; an open sentence with one unbound variable, such as 'x is white', can be satisfied by sequences of objects. And a sentence is just to be regarded as a sentential function with no unbound variables and so as a *zero-placed* sentential function. Tarski thus brings sentences which are capable of bearing truth values into the class of sentential functions which are capable of being satisfied by suitable objects. Such as extension of a concept to so-called 'degenerate cases' is a familiar and useful device in mathematics and logic. But we may naturally be suspicious of a device of this sort in an enterprise designed to define truth for empirical sentences. What sense, it may be asked, can be put on the concept of satisfaction for a zero-valued function when it has been defined and illustrated for functions whose values are one or more?

At this point Tarski brings into play another of the 'tricks' noted by Stegmüller. In his account of satisfaction, he considers first the cases of sentential functions containing only one or two free variables and then goes on to consider the general case where the function may contain an arbitrary number of free variables. In order not to have to take explicit account of the number of variables in any particular expression, he adopts the convention of assuming that 'a given infinite sequence of objects satisfies a given sentential function'.[57] He can then number the members of the sequence f and correspondingly number the variables of his system. The first member of the sequence will be correlated with the variable with the subscript 1, (x_1), the second member with the variable numbered 2 (x_2) and so on, the kth member being correlated with the kth variable. He can then *ignore* all the members of a sequence which are not correlated with any variable; and no account will be taken of them.

In examining the application of this second artifice, it is essential to bear in mind the crucial difference, for the semantic theory, between sentential functions (open sentences) which may be satisfied by some sequences and not by others and sentences which are either satisfied by all sequences or by none. In losing its variables, an expression shifts the range of its sensitivity to the objects which can satisfy it. In the end, it is satisfied by all or by none; and so is accounted either true or false. There are two ways in which an open sentence may be closed, as we have seen. It may have its variables bound by quantifiers or it may have them replaced by names of individuals.

In his formal exposition of the theory, Tarski considers only the first way of closing an open sentence, although he gives examples of the second. Let us look again at the way in which his requirements for satisfaction of a sentential function affect expressions with bound variables. (See page 97 above.) If a sentential function has a universal quantifier, the class variable bound by the quantifier (supposing that it is the kth), ranges over every class in any infinite sequence of classes that occupies the kth place in that sequence. Thus whereas an unquantified expression, say,

$$(x_m \subset x_n)$$

says that the mth class of a certain sequence is included in the nth, if we add a quantifier to get, say,

$$(Ax_m) \ (x_m \subset x_n)$$

this expression will be satisfied if and only if it would still be satisfied were f replaced by any other sequence differing from f only in having a different mth term. And this condition so narrows the possibilities of satisfaction that f would now satisfy $(Ax_m) \ (x_m \subset x_n)$ only if x_n were the universe class that includes all classes. So too in adding the second quantifier, we add a further restriction that makes it impossible for *any* infinite sequences of classes to satisfy the sentence with both variables bound. The outcome is that only if the original expression is *logically true* (and so satisfiable by all sequences) will the addition of quantifiers permit the resulting sentence still to be satisfied by all sequences and so to be true in the sense of the semantic theory. In any other case, the binding of all the variables of an open sentence results in a sentence satisfied by no sequence and so, on Tarski's definition, false. But to say that an expression is satisfied by all sequences is just to say that it is true under all possible conditions. Conversely, to say that a sentence is unsatisfiable by any range of circumstances is to say that it is logically false. But this is to fail to distinguish logical from factual truth.

It may be the case that this feature of the semantic theory is a consequence of the fact that Tarski's object language is the axiomatized class calculus. If this is so, perhaps another type of logical language may offer a more plausible medium for the logical reconstruction of the correspondence theory. However that may be, if the version of the semantic theory that we have considered does blur the border-line between logical and factual truth, it obviously fails to provide an adequate formulation of the basic ideas of the traditional notion of correspondence.

(e) This may be reinforced by one further point about satisfaction: 'it is easy to realise that whether or not a given sequence satisfies a given sentential function depends only on those terms of the sequence which correspond (in their indices) with the free variables of the function.' Thus the first term of the infinite sequence f corresponds with x_1, the second term with x_2 and so on. 'Thus in the extreme case, when the function is a sentence, and so contains no free variable (which is in no way excluded by Def. 22)* the satisfaction of a function by a sequence does not depend on the properties of the terms of the sequence at all. Only two possibilities remain: either every infinite sequence of classes satisfies a given sentence or no sequence satisfies it.'[58] Quine echoes the same point: 'Just as all but the first and second things in a sequence are irrelevant to "x conquered y" so all the things in a sequence are irrelevant to a sentence devoid of free variables.'[59]

But the correspondence theory of truth, of which the semantic theory claims to be a rational reconstruction, purports to explain the truth of empirical sentences. And it is a necessary condition of the success of an empirical sentence in conveying information about the world that its cognitive content should be descriptively adequate to the facts it pretends to communicate. Now if the claim of the semantic theory to be a clear restatement of the salvageable essence of the concept of correspondence is to be maintained, we have to ask what in the semantic theory are the analogues of (i) truth-bearers, (ii) facts and (iii) the relation of correspondence. The answers seem to be: (i) that sentences are the truth-bearers; (ii) that sequences of objects are the analogue of facts; (iii) that the relation of satisfaction between objects and sentences (open or closed) is the model for the relation of correspondence. But it turns out that items (ii) and (iii) of this analogy

*This is the four-part definition of satisfaction set out above on page 99.

are misleading. For satisfaction is defined for open sentences which are not truth-bearers and applies only vacuously to the bearers of truth values. And because it applies only vacuously, 'all the things in a sequence are irrelevant to a sentence devoid of free variables'.[60] This ruins the analogy, if ever it was intended, between facts and sequences of objects. For if there is one thing certain about facts, it is that they could never be irrelevant to the truth or falsity of sentences, in the everyday sense of 'truth' with which we are concerned. The conclusion must be that though the semantic theory of truth is a classical achievement in formal semantics, it has no relevance to the problem of empirical truth in everyday natural languages.

2 | States of affairs and semantic conventions

In recent years the most important discussion of the issues arising from the correspondence theory of truth have originated from the controversy between J. L. Austin and P. F. Strawson.[61] Austin sketched and defended a minimal version of the correspondence theory and Strawson's criticisms of this version have given rise to the most interesting developments in this area since Tarski's formulation of the semantic theory.

To say that a statement corresponds to the facts, according to Austin, 'can hardly be wrong. . . . Still it can be at least misleading.'[62] His version of this account of truth is designed to make explicit (a) exactly what is right about the statement and (b) what features of it can mislead us. In addition to the obvious essentials of a stock of symbols used and understood in a speech community and a world about which the symbols can convey information,

there must be two sets of conventions:
Descriptive conventions correlating the words (=sentences) with the *types* of situation, thing, event, etc., to be found in the world.
Demonstrative conventions correlating the words (=statements) with the *historic* situations etc., to be found in the world.[63]

(The significance of the switch from 'sentences' to 'statements' in this quotation is that 'statement' is used to refer to a sentence in its concrete context of utterance 'as used by a certain person on a certain occasion'.[64] For Austin, as for Strawson, it is statements that are truth-bearers, not sentences. This is one point, among several, on which Austin and Strawson both differ from Tarski.) Austin summarizes his version of the correspondence theory thus: 'A statement is said to be true when the historic state of affairs to which it is correlated by the demonstrative conventions (the one to which it 'refers') is of a type which the sentence used in making it is correlated by the descriptive conventions.'[65]

To this, he adds two caveats, one about the word 'fact' and one about 'corresponds'.

(a) It is easy to suppose, because of locutions like 'the fact that arsenic is poisonous', 'the fact that the Greeks defeated the Persians at Marathon' and so on, that 'fact' is synonymous with 'true statement'. But this is a mistake generated by the convenience of the English phrase 'the fact that . . .' in cases where we can usefully neglect the distinction between a true statement and what the statement is about or, more usually, what it says. Familiar language has a useful transparency which enables us to attend to the features of the world that we are talking of and not to the medium in which we talk. And ordinarily this is what we do. In other words, Austin is emphasizing that facts are objective features of the world. This is a point that we have earlier seen reason to query or at least to qualify; and it is a point that Strawson does not accept.

(b) Austin's second caveat (which Strawson does not dispute) is equally debatable. In order to avoid the difficulties of explaining correspondence in terms of any structural similarity of language to fact he goes to the other extreme.

The correlation between words (= sentences) and the type of situation, event, etc., which is to be such that when a statement in those words is made with reference to an historic situation of that type the statement is then true, is *absolutely and purely* conventional. We are absolutely free to appoint *any* symbol to describe *any* type of situation, so far as merely being true goes.[66]

This looks at first like a piece of solid commonsense. Of course, words are merely conventional and indeed arbitrary signs and so are the grammatical and syntactical rules that bind words together into sentences. So why should we not have what Austin calls 'a small one-spade language' in which 'nuts' was a statement which 'might be true in exactly the same circumstances as the statement in English that the National Liberals are the people's choice'.[67]

There is no need whatsoever [he continues] for the words used in making a true statement to 'mirror' in any way, however indirect, any

E

feature whatsoever of the situation or event; a statement no more needs, in order to be true, to reproduce the 'multiplicity' say, or the 'structure' or the 'form' of the reality, than a word needs to be echoic or writing pictographic. To suppose that it does, is to fall once again into the error of reading back into the world the features of language.[68]

Let us be clear what Austin is saying here. Contrast two hypothetical languages L_1 and L_2 with respect to four sentences.

English	L_1	L_2
The cat is on the mat	pag	pob
The dog is on the mat	pog	zim
The cat is on the sofa	pam	bap
The dog is on the sofa	pom	vun

Although we are not familiar with languages like L_1 it is clear that such a language does have a structure which in some way corresponds to the structure of the facts that can be stated in it. Some American Indian languages seem to be of this sort. (In his book *Language*, Sapir gives an instance of this type from Chinook.) But L_2 is a different matter altogether, as we shall see.

We do meet with examples of this type of symbolization in some systems of writing. Chinese, for example, has a script in which written signs stand directly for words with generally no indication of how the sign is to be pronounced. In languages with such scripts, we have to learn to read and write by direct association of the sign with the word. This is a much more laborious procedure than learning to read and write a language with an alphabetic or syllabic script. These scripts give us a system of rules by which we can compose or decipher words from their elements. Such a system of spelling rules is clearly enormously easier to learn than, say, the 1800 signs that the Japanese education authorities require from their secondary pupils.

But if Austin's extreme of conventionalism makes orthography difficult, it makes syntax impossible. It does not follow that because words can be arbitrarily associated with concepts and that rules of grammar and syntax are conventional in the sense that they vary in arbitrary ways from one group of languages to another, that therefore the association between truth-bearers and the situations that they represent is conventional in Austin's anarchic sense. Once we have adopted a set of syntactical rules, however arbitrary they may be, the rules, just because they are *rules,* impose a structure upon our language. There is a regularity about the ways in which we can indicate and comprehend such structural features of our universe of understanding as tense, modality, plurality, direction of action, topic of discussion and comment thereon and so on. Austin does belatedly recognize that 'a more developed language' has in its grammar and syntax characteristics that make it more learnable, adaptable, precise and so on; but, he insists, they 'do not make statements in it any more capable of being true or capable of being any more true'.[69]

One of the important features of natural languages that the work of Professor Noam Chomsky has brought to our attention is that a native speaker of, say, English can understand an indefinitely large number of sentences that he has never met before. Moreover he can construct for himself new sentences that he has never heard in the mouths of those from whom he has learned the language. A 'language' such as L_2 hypothesized above would not have this essential property of a natural language. In learning such a language, we should have to learn a separate word for each particular situation. And there would be no rules by which we could make up a word by which to refer to a situation that we had not met before. Thus Austin's hypothetical 'small one-spade language' lacks an essential feature of natural language. Austin's sentences would be, as it were, proper names for situations and events.

But why is this relevant to the correspondence theory of truth? It is relevant because the theory arises when we try to understand how *natural languages* work and how they convey to us the nature of the world. And although it is important to stress the conventional aspects of natural language, it is equally important, if we are to understand how truth is conveyed in such languages, that we should see clearly where convention is restricted by rule following. Although rules are conventions, it is part of the convention that they are followed. The fact that we are following a rule prevents us from adopting any convention that would involve behaviour inconsistent with our following that rule. In fact, there are two kinds of convention involved in using a natural language, those of the lexicon and those of syntax. Austin's 'small one-spade language' which he took to be the model case of convention following collapses syntax into the lexicon and so destroys the flexibility of the language not only for expressing meanings (as he admits) but also for conveying truth (which he does not admit).

Why would such a language, in spite of Austin's claim, be incapable of truth-stating? In the first place, it would be of use only for recording information and not for conveying it to someone who did not know it already. For a given statement S in the language L_2 could convey not, for example, that the cat is on the mat but only that this particular cat, here and now, is on this particular mat. Each statement would be bound to an individual space-time locus and could not express any feature that that particular state of affairs shared with other similar situations. The situation repeated would be referred to by quite a different expression. Thus the language would lack the generalizing function necessary for conveying meaning; and if it could not convey meaning, it clearly could not convey truth.

This failing is a direct consequence of the fact that the language lacks any internal structure. The structure of a simple sentence like:

50. The cat is on the mat

does more than relate features of the sentence to features of the world. It also relates the particular features of the situation described to features of other *similar* situations. 'Cat' refers to all cats as well as to this one; and so on. The truth-stating capacity of language is a consequence of its generalizing function.

Both Austin and, as we shall see, Strawson, try to separate the truth-bearing function of natural language from its meaning-load. In Austin's case, it is because he over-stresses the conventional nature of language; in the case of Strawson, it is for other reasons. Thus Austin's version of the correspondence theory of truth is simple and straightforward. Language has, for this purpose, two principal functions. It can *describe types* of things and events and it can *indicate particular* things and events. For truth-stating, these two ways of working, the generalizing and the particularizing, are combined so that 'a statement is said to be true when the historic state of affairs to which it is correlated by the demonstrative conventions (the one to which it "refers") is of a type with which the sentence used in making it is correlated by the descriptive conventions'.[70]

Strawson calls this a 'purified' version of the correspondence theory and seems to accept two features of it, (a) the affixing of the predicate 'true' to statements rather than, as the semantic theory does, to sentences; (b) the emphasis on the purely conventional nature of the relation of correspondence which implies a rejection of any kind of structural correspondence between the world and language. His objections to it concern two principal points: (a) that as a theory of truth it is too narrowly concerned with a special type of simple fact-stating statements; (b) that it is in any case not so much a theory of truth as an inadequate theory of meaning, 'an incipient analysis of the statement-making use of language'.[71] He believes that 'the correspondence theory requires, not purification, but elimination'.[72] But his criticism of Austin's account is not simply destructive. It raises a number of subtle and important insights into truth and meaning and the connections between them.

Strawson's own account of truth is in part a criticism of Austin's views and in part a positive statement of his own. The criticism of Austin was put forward in two stages, the first in the Aristotelian symposium of 1950 and the second in 1965 in response to a paper by Mr G. J. Warnock.[73] In his original paper, he was very largely concerned with the objective term of the correspondence relation, variously referred to by Austin as 'thing', 'event', 'situation', 'feature', 'state of affairs' and 'fact'.

In the first place, it is essential to distinguish between 'what the statement is about' and what makes the statement true. The first element is the person, thing, class of objects or event which the statement is about, the *topic* of discussion or subject. A statement refers to the topic and offers a description of it. Indeed, simple statements are 'just reference-cum-description'.[74] The reference may be correct or incorrect; the description may fit or fail to fit its subject. But the subjects (the persons, things or events referred to) by the referring part of the statement and described, fittingly or otherwise, by the describing part are not the *fact*. 'The only plausible candidate for the position of what (in the world) makes the statement true is the fact it states; but the fact it states is not something in the world.'[75]

Thus Strawson's first objection to Austin is that to talk of what statements are about and of what makes them true is not just to use different language for referring to the same features of the world. Facts are not features of the world as are the things and events which our statements refer to and describe. To suppose that they are is 'a logically fundamental type-mistake'.[76] Thus if I say:

  75. There is a bay tree in my garden

my statement of 75 refers to the bay tree and describes it by saying that it is in my garden. It does this, as Austin says, in virtue of the demonstrative and descriptive conventions of the language that I use. But *the fact that* there is a bay tree in my garden which is what makes my utterance of 75 a true statement is not something that is either described or referred to as is the tree that I am talking about. That statements can 'fit the facts' is not evidence that facts are features of the world. 'Of course, statements and facts fit. They were made for each other. If you prize the statements off the world you prize the facts off it too; but the world would be none the poorer.'[77]

Before we go on to consider what Strawson's objections to Austin's use of 'facts' amounts to, it is worth emphasizing that a linguistic expression can very well meet Austin's criterion of satisfying the descriptive and demonstrative conventions of our language without at the same time qualifying for a truth value. A descriptive expression like 'the tall girl in the green dress standing by the door' picks out the object of our reference by a combination of description and demonstration. But since it is not a statement, it is neither true nor false, though it could, of course, be appraised as apt or inapt, appropriate or misleading in virtue of its descriptive or its designative powers. This shows that Austin's conditions for truth of a statement may be necessary but are clearly not sufficient. We have earlier made the distinction between expressions which are 'true of' the world, or weakly true, and those *statements* which are true or false in a stronger sense. Only sentences which are asserted can have a truth value though unasserted sentences or even descriptive phrases like the one cited above may have a weak approximation to truth in being descriptively adequate to one or more features of the world. We might say, of them, perhaps, that they are 'potentially true' in that they have an appropriate locus of application but that they do not qualify for the title of true or false until they have been applied to this locus by an act of assertion.

But these are not Strawson's reasons for rejecting Austin's

account of truth. He believes that facts are not the sort of entities that can be described or referred to. And that they cannot is not due to practical difficulties brought about, perhaps, by the inadequacy of language. It is rather that facts cannot *logically* be described or referred to. Given that a statement has what Strawson calls a 'referring part' which designates those individual features of the world which the statement is about and a 'describing part' which purports to attribute properties to those features 'it is evident that there is nothing else in the world for the statement itself to be related to either in some further way of its own or in either of the different ways in which these different parts of the statement are related to what the statement is about'.[78] Moreover, 'the demand that there should be such relatum is logically absurd'.

This objection is stated somewhat cryptically by Strawson; and it is easier to understand what he is claiming than to see his reasons for the claim. 'Facts are what statements (when true) state; they are not what statements are about.'[79] What statements are about are the things and events in the world and their properties and relations; what they state is *that* such and such things and events have such and such properties. But the fact that a statement states is not itself 'something in the world'. This tells us what facts are not; but how are we to understand what they are? For Strawson does not want to maintain any such absurd position as that there are no facts. In any case, we could still deny that there 'is nothing else in the world for the statement itself to be related to' if we were to adopt a Russellian view of facts as the qualifying of a thing by a property or the relating of two or more things by a relation. For then we could admit that a statement referred to those things of which it predicated properties or relations and claim that the fact was simply the total situation conveyed by the statement. The elements of the situation are referred to and described; the fact itself is conveyed. On this interpretation, facts would be the material counterpart of the cognitive content of indicative statements.

However, though this account could be developed to accommodate a disciple of Russell, it is open to serious objections. Consideration of these objections goes some way to support Strawson's view of a fact to which a statement is said to correspond as being 'the *pseudo*material correlate of the statement as a whole'.[80] The prefix 'pseudo' here is intended to convey that the term 'fact' makes a claim to an objectivity and an independence of human judgement that cannot be justified. We have seen earlier that on a traditional correspondence account of truth general and negative statements require general and negative facts to stand as their objective counterparts. Intractable to our understanding as these notions are, the straightforward indicative singular statements typified by 'The cat is on the mat' present less obvious but equally serious difficulties. Because our concepts are embodied in general words, they are as much reflections of our linguistic apparatus as they are informative about the real world. Sapir's words, quoted earlier, have abundant empirical support: 'The fact of the matter is that the "real world" is to a large extent built up on the language habits of the group. . . . We see and hear and otherwise experience very largely as we do because the language habits of our community predispose certain choices of interpretation.' It is considerations like these more than any others that give the strongest support to Strawson's views on the status of facts.

If we grant, as we must, that the word 'fact' does not stand for features of or elements in a material world whose nature and existence owes nothing to human minds, we have still to say what it does stand for. And here we must proceed carefully. We do not want to avoid the crudities of Russellian commonsense at the cost of endorsing the fantasies of objective idealism.

Let us grant then (a) that an indicative statement designates those features of the world that it simultaneously describes; (b) that the complex of 'individual-cum-properties' so designated and described is not a fact; (c) that there is nothing else *in the world* with which the statement has any semantic relation. If then there is no semantic relation between statement and fact, there can be no question of a statement even to be logically capable of corresponding with fact. For facts are on the wrong side of the semantic fence to be candidates for correspondence. This raises two questions: (i) what coherent account are we to give of facts? (ii) does it follow from this deportation of facts from the material to the conceptual world that there is nothing *in the world* which can stand as what Strawson calls 'the material correlate' of the statement?

The earlier discussion of the nature of facts was largely concerned to say what facts were *not* and gave only loose and meta-phorical hints as to what they *were*. Let us see if anything more positive can be said of them.

We may start from a remark made earlier to the effect that a fact might be interpreted as being the objective or material counterpart of the cognitive content of an indicative statement. The principal object to this is, as we saw, that the conceptual map of the world which is drawn in the lexicon and the syntax of any natural language may well not reflect the actual make-up of the world. Changes in our conceptual model of the world are brought about piecemeal by the advance of knowledge, in particular, the advance of the natural sciences. And the prudent and rational man will always be aware that there are gaps and inaccuracies in the conceptual map which his native language presents him with. This means that we have no guarantee that the cognitive content of any particular statement reliably maps that area of the world to which our assertion assigns it. Let us then amend this account of fact to read: a fact is simply the cognitive content of an indicative statement. This transfers facts across the semantic border into the realm of language where, it seems, Strawson would want to locate them.

But clearly it will not do as it stands. For false statements have as much cognitive content as true ones. And it is just because false statements do not convey the facts to us that we have no use for them. Let us then amend our account further so that it reads: a fact is the cognitive content of a true statement. This version does indeed have some advantages. It is, in fact, Straw-son's view that 'facts are what statements (when true) state'. And it makes clear why it is 'a logically fundamental type-mistake' to postulate the existence of something in the world which makes a statement true. For if a fact is just the cognitive content of a true statement, the statement cannot be true in virtue of facts. For no *empirical* statement can be true in virtue of its own meaning.

But this account of facts does have some awkward consequences. For example, if we are to understand that a statement is a sentence used to make an assertion, there would be no facts in the absence of language. This is a consequence that Strawson seems content to accept. 'Of course,' he says, 'statements and facts fit. They were made for each other. If you prize the statements off the world you would prize the facts off it too; but the world would be none the poorer.'[81] It is extremely difficult to talk coherently about the nature of facts for the obvious reason that innocent-sounding phrases like 'what the sentence says' are ambiguous in just the way that occasions the difficulty that we are trying to resolve. What we refer to and describe is presented to us in a symbolic form that seems at once transparent in that we see through the words to the world and opaque in that we see the world only in the conceptual dress of language. This makes us try, in Professor Davidson's words, 'to include in the entity to which a true sentence corresponds not only the objects the sentence is "about" (another idea full of trouble) but also whatever the sentence says about them'.[82] But what could be more natural than to assume that language must be fact-conveying as well as fact-expressing? For if it were not, we have to believe that a world without language is also a world without facts.

A part of this difficulty arises because of the loose and ambiguous ways in which 'fact'* is used in ordinary English. In one quite usual sense of the word, 'fact' *is* used in the Russell–McTaggart sense of an objective mind-independent state of affairs. 'You can't ignore the facts' and similar well-known locutions takes the word in this sense. But we cannot talk about, describe, record or otherwise express these facts in language without transmitting them into Strawsonian facts which are the cognitive contents of true statements. If we hear that the disciplinary committee has examined the facts of the case, we understand that the committee has read transcripts of evidence or listened to the statements of witnesses and so on. They were considering the meaning-content of (putatively) true statements.

We could evade this tiresome ambiguity by reserving phrases like 'situations' or 'states of affairs' for the Russell–McTaggart sense of 'fact'. (And Strawson admits that these are 'more plausible candidates for inclusion in the world'.)[83] We may then continue to use 'fact' in Strawson's more defensible sense. But if facts are just 'what statements (when true) state', we cannot recognize a fact for what it is until we have verified the statement which embodies it. But why does this matter? It means merely that facts are no longer of interest in the search for a realist theory of truth. Cognitive contents of empirical statements are all candi-

*See Austin's appeal to the *Oxford English Dictionary*, 'Unfair to Facts' in *Philosophical Papers* (Oxford, 1961).

dates for the status of fact; but they can only be accorded the status after the statement has been verified.

Fifteen years after his original paper, Strawson returned to his criticism of Austin's thesis in a paper of formidable subtlety.[84] He develops three principal objections to Austin's original thesis. In the first place, he argues that Austin's distinction between the descriptive conventions of language and the demonstrative conventions cannot be maintained. Strawson does not deny that there are two linguistic *functions* which may be distinguished as descriptive and demonstrative but he does deny that there is any corresponding duality of conventions. For surely it is the case that the so-called descriptive uses of language may also serve to fix a particular utterance as referring to a given situation. If demonstrative conventions 'correlate particular utterances of sentences (or: correlate words as uttered on particular occasions) with particular historical situations'[85] it is obvious that descriptive conventions also play a part in correlating particular utterances with particular occasions. Indeed, it is clear that just as we can make a description of a given individual so detailed that it can apply only to that individual and to no other, so we could, if it were worth the trouble, describe a situation in such close detail that our description could fit only that one situation. Strawson does not make this claim; but it is surely the case that descriptive uses of language can provide substitutes, even if inconvenient ones, for designative uses in this way. If this is so, Austin's dichotomy of semantics cannot plausibly be defended.

It might well be claimed, however, by a defender of Austin's position that there are some words and phrases in all languages which are uniquely suited to designating situations and events without describing them. These are such words as 'here', 'there', 'now' and similar indexing adverbials of time and place, together with phrases indicating space-time co-ordinates, 'latitude 17° 18′N, longitude 62° 48′W, 22 hrs GMT 22 April 1975'. Such locutions have a minimal descriptive content and a maximal designative function. But even in such cases, it cannot be said that there is no descriptive sense at all. Spatial and temporal predicates are, after all, predicates. 'Here' is a spatial pointer and 'now' is a temporal one. Moreover, phrases assigning latitude, longitude and time must presuppose a reference to a co-ordinate system such as the equator, the Greenwich meridian, the birth of Christ and so on.

And the origins of the co-ordinate system have to be assigned by description.

Let us allow, as Strawson does, that we may evade the difficulties arising from talking of demonstrative conventions and descriptive conventions by referring to both types together as 'semantic conventions'. He now notes a second difficulty: Austin makes an indefensible use of the notion of the historical situation to which a statement must refer. Let us suppose, with Austin, that a statement cannot be true unless it refers to the identical historical situation which it also describes. If we do this, we use the notion of a given historical situation to explain what it means to say that a given statement is true. Now either we can identify this situation without reference to the statement or we cannot. If we cannot so identify it, we have the absurd consequence that every factual statement is true. Let us suppose then that we can identify the situation without reference to the statement in question. But how *could* we do this? Any objectively given spatio-temporal chunks of the world can only be identified as particular states of affairs under some description which picks out their identifying features and maps out their limits. Thus it is impossible to identify a given situation independently of a linguistic or other conceptual specification. If these alternatives are exhaustive, it appears that the concept of 'historical situation', like that of 'fact' (and for similar reasons) is on the wrong side of the semantic divide to serve as part of the explanation of the concept of truth.

Lastly, Strawson objects that the notion of semantical conventions 'correlating' states of affairs with expressions is far too vague to be at all explanatory of the notion of truth. What such conventions govern is the meaning-load or cognitive content of statements. Semantical conventions are no less relevant to the false statement:

76. Tigers are found in Africa

than they are to the true statement:

77. Tigers are not found in Africa

In short, semantical conventions account for *meaning* and not for *truth*.

There are indeed other objections to Austin's attempted re-formulation of the traditional correspondence theory of truth.

For example, it is not clear how it could be plausibly applied to negative or general statements. But however this may be, Strawson's critique justifies his claim that Austin fails 'to distinguish between the task of elucidating the nature of a certain type of communication (the empirically informative) from the problem of the actual functioning of the word "true" within the framework of that type of communication'.[86] What Austin does succeed in doing is to specify some of the necessary conditions for correctly declaring a statement to be true.

But what of Strawson's positive account of truth? In an early paper[87] he comes near to endorsing the view of truth put forward by F. P. Ramsey: 'It is evident that "It is true that Caesar was murdered" means no more than that Caesar was murdered, and "It is false that Caesar was murdered" means that Caesar was not murdered.'[88] This brisk account of truth and falsity, sometimes known as the Redundancy Theory has a certain superficial attraction on the ground that the conditions which justify us in assenting to P are identical with those which justify assent to 'P is true'; and similarly for 'not-P' and 'P is false'. But these considerations alone are insufficient. As Professor A. R. White has observed, logical equivalence is not the same as equivalence of meaning[89] and Ramsey's case for the redundancy theory does no more than establish the logical equivalence of 'P' with 'P is true'.

Strawson's original verdict on this account was that it was true but inadequate. It is 'right in asserting that to say that a statement is true is not to make a further statement; but wrong in suggesting that to say that a statement is true is not to do something different from, or additional to, just making the statement'.[90] If I say 'That's true' in response to some statement that you have made 'I am in a manner making an assertion, namely, the assertion you made'.[91] But, in addition, I am confirming or admitting what you have said. It is this confirmatory or concessive use of 'true' which is its most important feature, a diagnosis which Strawson thinks is supported by the actual use of the word 'true' in everyday discourse.

Later, in response to criticism by Mr G. J. Warnock in his paper 'A Problem about Truth', Strawson amended his own account of truth a little though only to the extent of conceding that to say of a statement S that it is true or false *is* to make a further statement about the original S. This concession does seem to be at variance with the dictum entrenched in Strawson's original position: 'Truth is not a property of symbols; for it is not a property.'[92] For he now concedes that the phrase 'is true' is a predicate and on the reasonable assumption that predicates are the verbal expressions of properties, truth must be a property. But in the paper in which he replies to Warnock[93] he contents himself with showing that even if what he now calls 'the undisputed thesis' that 'is true' can be used to make a statement about a statement is accepted it is as consistent with Strawson's own Ramsey-like account of truth as it is with the Austinian theory which Warnock favours.

But even if we concede that Strawson's conversion to 'the undisputed thesis' raises no problems for his version of the redundancy theory, there are other objections still to be faced. The essential feature of his version is that using words like 'true', 'false' and their synonyms and cognates functions as a device for assertion (or denial). And since the assertion is parasitic on another statement already made, to say that a statement is true is to acknowledge, admit or concede what is said rather than to describe the statement as having a certain property or relation. I shall make two points about this account.

(a) It cannot be denied that a phrase like 'That's true' can be used in English in the concessive sense that Strawson emphasizes. In such uses, the phrase could serve as a substitute for 'I agree', 'that's so', 'yes' or, in the American vernacular, 'right'. But the question obviously arises whether Strawson's point is a *linguistic* one peculiar to English and perhaps a few other languages or whether it is a philosophical truth which holds in all languages. Even if we grant the value of linguistic methods in philosophy, any conscientious practitioner of such methods must surely raise the question: 'parochially linguistic or common to all languages?' about any candidate for philosophical truth that he may wish to support. A doubt has been raised about this particular candidate by Professor Stegmüller who observes that German-speaking philosophers find that Strawson's suggestion about the function of 'That's true' in English is not perfectly mirrored by the way

Das ist wahr works in German.[94] In many contexts, the German phrase would sound unacceptably exaggerated, strained or unusual, if used as a substitute for *Ja* or *Genau*.

It is clear that the only way to test Strawson's hypothesis (for it *is* a hypothesis and fortunately a falsifiable one) is to take a sufficiently large and varied sample of opinions on analogous linguistic usages from native speakers of a wide range of languages. This would be a formidable experiment in the sociology of language, calling for the collaboration of experts in different fields. For what it is worth, the results of a small pilot survey of twenty languages that I have made are not uniformly favourable to Strawson's thesis, although the favourable cases, especially in the Indo-European family, outweigh the counter-examples.

(b) But there is a more substantial objection. Suppose we grant that Strawson is right in claiming that 'true' functions in English as what he calls 'an abbreviatory statement device' which serves to indicate our endorsement of an assertion. (Similarly, 'false' operates characteristically to signify our rejection of an assertion.) The question then arises: in virtue of what supposed properties do we endorse or reject statements? We may no longer say that it is because they seem to us true (or false) for these terms have now been assigned to other duties. But any rational person has to give some answer to this question. And it is this very question that raises the interesting problem for the theory of knowledge that was once, in pre-Strawsonian days, called 'the problem of truth'. It does not much matter what terms we substitite for the lost 'true' and 'false'. We could talk of assertions being 'well founded' or 'accurate' or 'groundless' or 'inaccurate'; or we could substitute Dewey's 'warranted assertibility' for 'truth'; or we could use 'T' and 'F' in the manner of the logic books. Whatever labels of acceptability or its opposite we applied to beliefs and statements, we would still have to defend our assignment of these labels by reference to some rational criteria. So we are left with our problem.

Thus Strawson's work on the problem of truth has two sides, negative and positive. The negative side is a largely successful attack on a promising contemporary version of the correspondence theory. The positive side evades the problem.

3 | Conclusion

In the first part of this book, we surveyed the difficulties in the way of making a clear and consistent philosophical theory out of a commonsense conviction—that true beliefs and statements correspond to facts. We saw that once we try to make that harmless-sounding piece of commonsense explicit, we meet serious problems. What kinds of entities are to be called true or false—beliefs, propositions, judgements, statements, sentences? What are facts? What exactly is the relation that we optimistically christen 'correspondence'? It is a precondition of stating and justifying a version of the correspondence theory of truth that we find clear and consistent answers to these questions. So far as our investigations went, such answers were not to be found. We then examined the semantic theory of truth which has been claimed by its exponents to be a rational reconstruction of the essential ideas of the traditional notion of truth as correspondence. But this theory, whatever its merits as an explication of the concept of truth in formalized languages, seemed to be a very poor approximation to the traditional correspondence account of the truth of empirical statements.

The Austin–Strawson controversy, on the other hand, centred on issues crucial to the traditional theory and raised serious doubts about the role played by the concept of 'fact' in Austin's version of the theory and about the explanatory function of the semantic conventions linking language to the world. However, as he himself explains, Strawson sees the problem of truth from an unusual angle:

The occurrence *in ordinary discourse* of the words 'true', 'fact', etc., signalizes, without commenting on, the occurrence of a certain way of using language. When we use these words in ordinary life, we are talking within, and not about, a certain frame of discourse: we are precisely not talking about the way in which utterances are, or may be, conventionally related to the world. [95]

This point of view accounts for the fact which I suggested as a criticism of Strawson's own Ramsey-type theory: he seems unwilling to raise (or uninterested in raising) the question *why* we assent to some statements and reject others. This would be to talk *about* the frame of reference within which we use the terms 'true' and 'false'. But he has not shown that attempts to talk in this way must always be radically misguided. All he has shown is that Austin's attempt to talk in this way is open to a number of disabling objections. Indeed, to object in principle to such attempts would be to reject as illegitimate many problems in the theory of knowledge and the philosophy of language. In particular semantics would become an illusory enterprise. Thus underlying Strawson's particular (and very valuable) criticisms of a promising version of the correspondence theory is the conviction that all such theories are basically misconceived. ('The correspondence theory requires, not purification, but elimination.') [96]

But if we believe that the study of ordinary discourse is only one way among others to philosophical enlightenment, we need not be discouraged by the outcome of the Austin–Strawson controversy. Let us return then to the question of the nature of facts and, accepting Strawson's placing of facts on the linguistic side of the semantic divide, try to take the argument further. Let us admit that a fact is the cognitive content of a true empirical statement, in Strawson's phrase, 'what statements (when true) state'. (The occurrence of the word 'true' here is disconcerting as it is not obviously consistent with Strawson's own account of truth; but we may waive this point as a side issue.) Why may not the defender of a correspondence theory merely alter his terminology: a true statement is one which corresponds with the situation or state of affairs which is stated to obtain in the world? States of affairs are things characterized by properties or groups of things linked by relations; and languages are systems of morphemes ordered by rules of syntax. Here we have two systems, sub-systems of which may perhaps be shown on occasion to be structurally similar to each other. Indeed, it is now *facts*, in our reformed sense, which are held to correspond to states of affairs. They are so held when the language in which the content of the statement is expressed is structurally similar to the situation

or state of affairs to which the statement is assigned by its utterance. (We may postpone, for the moment, the question of the
nature of this hypothesized 'structural similarity'.)

The answer to this must be the same as before. We may not
simply re-title facts as 'states of affairs', 'situations' or some
equally objective-sounding equivalent. For what we count as
objects, properties, situations, relations and so on are equally
features of the world as seen in our conceptual mirror. Once we
have accepted the enormous advantages of language, we are
incapable of seeing the world untainted by those very concepts
that enable us to order and understand it. We have here something like a modern version of Plato's cave.[97] The shadows that
we cave-dwellers see are features of the world indeed, but
features selected and processed by the conceptual apparatus
with which our senses, memory and language have endowed us.
We can never turn to examine the objects that cast the shadows.

Nevertheless, we are not hopelessly imprisoned by our own
concepts in some old-fashioned idealist nightmare. But in order
to map out the limits of our freedom in this regard, we need an
addition to our vocabulary that is not conceptually tainted. In
order to refer in neutral terms to the raw unexperienced welter
of objects and events I shall use the Latin phrase *status rerum*.*

We could then propose a hypothesis, or rather, a schema for
hypotheses to provide a minimal basis for a correspondence
theory of truth. The universe of discourse for the theory has
three parts:

A. *status rerum*
B. things and their properties, situations, events
C. empirical statements

The links between B and C are the semantic conventions (for a
given language). The links between A and B are the cognitive
processes of sensation, perception, memory and concept formation. B is a selectively processed and edited version of *status
rerum*; C is a selectively processed and edited version of B.

The truth relation links A with C; so it is clear that semantic
conventions alone cannot account for truth. Their task is to

---

*This term has a respectable philosophical ancestry in that it was suggested
by Wittgenstein to C. K. Ogden as a suitable translation for '*Sachlage*' for
the *Tractatus*. The suggestion was, of course, not adopted.[98]

explain meaning, which is a necessary condition for truth (and for falsity as well). But if any statements are to be true (and we know that some are) there must be features of *status rerum* that are transmissible to statements in such a way that we can use the statements as reliable surrogates for and guides to *status rerum*. Thus language must be in some sense a trustworthy map or model of the unconceptualized world. And if X is a model or map of Y, it must share some of the structural features of Y. The schema of hypotheses referred to above is that there are structural features of *status rerum* which are conceptually and linguistically transmissible. Exactly what such features are will depend in the first place on our sensory apparatus and our powers of conceptualizing. This accounts for the transmission of structure from A to B and this is why the world (that is, the B-world) of dogs, insects or intelligent creatures from outer space would be very different from our own; and why the world of Newton, Shakespeare or Mozart is different from that of savages or mental defectives. But what features are then conveyed by semantic rules from B to C will be determined by the syntax and lexicon of the language in which the empirical statements are expressed.

Thus the salvable essence of the correspondence theory of truth is reduced to the modest hypothesis-schema that *some* of the structural features of *status rerum* can be transmitted to us in conceptual and linguistic form. But why is this a schema and what are the hypotheses?

It is a schema because it gives rise to an indefinite number of hypotheses of the form: This statement S is a model of some aspect of *status rerum*. And the hypotheses are genuine (because falsifiable). 'True' in this context is equivalent to 'is a model of some aspect of *status rerum*'. I can corroborate or disconfirm the hypothesis that S is a true statement, in the first place, by pragmatic tests of workability. Is the assumption that S mirrors some structural features of *status rerum* borne out, to some degree at least, by further experience? and, if it passes these pragmatic tests, is it consistent with the body of accepted knowledge? Thus the coherence and the pragmatic accounts of truth, though they notoriously fail as theories of the nature of truth, can at least provide tests to pass or fail particular candidates for the category of true statement.

It is worth looking further at these two types of correspondence. The naive type of correspondence theory which talks of correspondence between language (or 'thought') and 'reality' fails to comment on an important and obvious feature of such a relation. *Status rerum,* the unconceptualized flux of things and events is vastly more complex, dense and populous than the sparse selection from its riches that our conceptualized B-world presents us with. The cognitive powers of conscious creatures, though they differ very widely from one species to another and from individual to individual, are incapable of providing us with more than a small (and perhaps unrepresentative) sample in a cognizable form. This is because our sense organs are responsive only to certain types of energy and only to limited spectra of those types. The human eye, for example, is sensitive to only a tiny range of the electromagnetic spectrum and the human ear to a small range of sound. And there are many forms of energy to which we are not sensitive at all and which we can know of only when scientific ingenuity has translated them (by galvanometers, spectrographs, oscilloscopes, electron microscopes and so on) into forms which our sense organs can assimilate. Moreover, the cognitive apparatus by which we process and store this sensory information is limited by the structure and complexity of our central nervous systems. The human brain with its 10^{10} neurons has told us a lot about the universe; but if it was larger and more complex, it could tell us a great deal more. Thus the B-world of our concepts is not a picture of *status rerum*; it is rather a very primitive map which picks out in a crude way just those few features of the raw universe which our evolutionary history has endowed us to make use of.

When we move from the B-world to the world of language, this selective process continues. The generalizing function of language, which is essential to its ability to carry and convey information, requires it to neglect the concrete and particular character of the world of our experience along with its multitudinous variety. A workable language may have quite a small vocabulary to deal with those features of the world which interest and engage us. But the richness of experience, which even the B-world offers, cannot be conveyed by the lexicon and syntax of a natural language.

Thus in both these moves, from *status rerum* to the conceptualized world of experience and from that to the world of language, there is a successive selection and impoverishment of content and variety. Language cannot represent the whole of reality to us but only, at best, an extract from a sample. These considerations are obvious enough though they have been under-regarded by writers about truth.

Two points that have been raised earlier deserve mention. The first is the question of beliefs unexpressed in language; the second is the distinction between the strong and the weak sense of 'true'.

(a) If we postulate the B-world of conscious creatures, we can at least talk about, if not solve, the problem of the truth value of inarticulate and unexpressed beliefs. This is a problem for anyone who wants to preserve some minimum content for the correspondence theory because of our natural tendency to look on beliefs expressed in language as standard and to account for their truth or falsity in terms of the meaning rules which co-ordinate language with the B-world of inarticulate experience. Correspondence here is a matter of matching, however loosely, the structure of language with that of experience. But, as we have seen, the truth or falsity of unexpressed beliefs is prior, both in an evolutionary sense and in our individual experience, to that of beliefs expressed in language. Correspondence at this level is a question of the links between those features of *status rerum* that are accessible to us in virtue of our cognitive powers and the stable conceptual features of our pre-linguistic experience. The mapping of this difficult area is a task for collaboration between the psychology and the philosophy of cognition. And it is, as yet, in a very primitive state. We can say, indeed, that the isomorphism of *status rerum* and the B-world of pre-linguistic experience is of a different kind from that between language and the B-world. The writ of semantics has no authority here. It is the old problem of Kant's noumena and the world of experience in a slightly more tractable form.

(b) A propositional form of words may be weakly true if it is a descriptively adequate expression with reference to a certain situation but is not actually affirmed of that situation. The strong sense of 'true' is used of those expressions which are both descriptively adequate and actually affirmed. In other words, we have two necessary conditions for the strong sense of truth: (i) the expression S is descriptively adequate in that it satisfies the semantic conventions of the language; (ii) S is actually affirmed or asserted.

If we are prepared to say anything conclusive about the strong sense of 'true', we have to be prepared to give some account of assertion. We must also be prepared to show that (a) and (b) above are jointly sufficient conditions as well as being separately necessary or else add some further conditions. However, so far as concerns the correspondence theory of truth, we need not worry about these matters. If we are attending to propositions expressed in language (or in some conventional form of symbolic notation) the structural similarity of S to *status rerum*, however explained, will not be affected in any way whether S is asserted or not. Only if assertion is to be regarded as in some way *internal* to the statement would the structure of the statement be affected and so differ from that of an unasserted statement.

However, it is easy to show that the concept of assertion cannot be so regarded. Let us use the term 'proposition' here for whatever is asserted when we make a statement. It is clear that I can entertain or contemplate a proposition P without asserting it. I may, for example, be considering a hypothesis or wondering if there is adequate evidence to support the proposition. If I decide that P is worthy of belief, I may then assert it. But in doing so I do not change its content. For if I did I would not be asserting that same P which I had decided to be worthy of belief. Similarly, if A agrees to a statement S made by B, he is assenting to S and not to the proposition 'B says S' or 'S and B says S'. Thus assertion does not change the content of a statement, although it does make a proposition into a statement.

Clearly then, assertion is in no way internal to a statement. If it were, of course, the distinction that I made between strongly true and weakly true would be untenable. Suppose then that when I assert P, my assertion has nothing to do with the cognitive content of what is being asserted. What then is my assertion? There are two plausible answers.

(a) Assertion is a *mental act* on the part of the person who makes the assertion. In asserting P, I accept P as true and evince my acceptance. (Note that this is not a circular explanation. We need the notion of assertion to explain the concept of *strongly true*. In saying that I accept P as true, I mean 'true' in the sense of *weakly true* or descriptively adequate.) Objections to such an account would rest on objections to the very notion of a mental act. There have been plenty of such objections in contemporary philosophy; but whatever they may be worth, they have no bearing on the notion of truth as correspondence.

(b) Assertion is a *speech act*, that is to say, a conventional rule-governed social use of language. Other such uses of the same generic type but of different species are promising, warning, commanding, questioning and many others.[99] A full explication of the concept of asserting as a speech act would probably have to include the intentions of the person making the assertion. This might, depending on the way in which we analyse 'intention', overlap with the mental act account. There have been powerful criticisms of the notion of a speech act but we need not consider them here. Whatever their force, assertion viewed in this way can have no connection with the notion of truth as correspondence. For that concerns only the transmission of information from *status rerum* to the beliefs or statements that are held to embody it when we classify them as true.

This account of the correspondence theory may seem unadventurous to the point of banality. It reduces the theory to a trivial and indeed truistic statement amounting to no more than something like: language and beliefs can be informative. Is not that just a tautology? Perhaps this is so. But after all, truisms and tautologies are at least true; and they are often neglected. Moreover it does show that the metaphor of 'correspondence' is not a completely empty one and that Austin's idea of a totally conventional relation between language and the unconceptualized world is quite mistaken. It shows us further the areas in which we are to look for the correspondence relation; and that there is one type of correspondence between A and B of our universe of discourse and another between B and C. That between B and C is the proper field for semantics or the theory of meaning. That between A and B is a field for the psychology and philosophy of cognition—sensation, perception and concept-formation. All this raises philosophical issues of great complexity.

Although the division of correspondence into these two varieties has to be recognized, we have also to admit that, as we saw earlier, it is not possible to make a perfectly clear division between the world as conceptualized and the world as expressed in language. Many concepts cannot exist without language. But unless we are to deny truth values to inarticulate beliefs, and concepts to infants or animals, we must concede the reality of B, the non-linguistic but conceptualized world of things, properties, relations, events and situations. In practice, of course, human language learning starts at so early an age that there is a constant interplay between language learning and the formation of concepts. But unless small children had some system of pre-linguistic concepts, they could hardly begin to learn their native language.

So the old-fashioned problem of the correspondence of thought with reality is not a self-contained issue. There are two varieties of the correspondence relation, one of which turns out to be the problem of meaning and the other, more basic and more difficult, that of the origins and limits of empirical knowledge. Whatever the detailed structure of such relations of correspondence may turn out to be, no short answer can be given to the questions they raise. In so far as our brief concerns the correspondence theory of truth, we can say that we have divided the issue into two and assigned it to other philosophical areas. At least, however, we can see that truth is not, in the scholastic phrase, *adaequatio intellectus et rei*. It is just the tenuous link between consciousness and *status rerum* which enables us, and all other animals, to live successfully in the world and even, sometimes, to enjoy it. But, to adapt the verdict on art immortalized by Professor Goodman,[100] 'Truth is not a copy of the real world. One of the damn things is enough.'

Notes and references

References are to the items of the bibliography.

1. Russell (1912), chapter xii.
2. O'Connor (1968).
3. e.g. Price (1934).
4. Price (1969).
5. Hamlyn (1971).
6. Strawson (1971), pages 1–27.
7. Geach (1965).
8. Ryle (1930).
9. Carnap (1951), pages 27ff.
10. Leonard (1967), page 47.
11. Chomsky (1972), pages 16ff.
12. Hockett (1958).
13. Chomsky (1972), pages 28–9.
14. Quine (1969).
15. Quine (1970), page 13.
16. Quine (1960), page 190.
17. Quine (1960).
18. Quine (1970), chapter 1.
19. Russell (1914), page 60.
20. Russell (1956), page 285.
21. Russell (1956), page 214.
22. von Senden (1960).
23. e.g. Wittgenstein's *Tractatus Logico-Philosophicus*, on most interpretations of that ambiguous classic.
24. e.g. E. H. Lenneberg in Fodor and Katz (1964).
25. Russell (1949), chapter 25.
26. Sapir (1931).
27. Whorf (1956).
28. Kluckhohn and Leighton (1946), page 182.
29. For a contemporary discussion, with references, see Penn (1972).
30. The Nootka language is spoken by a tribe of Indians in one of the coastal regions of British Columbia. Whorf takes a simple English sentence:

    (A) He invites people to a feast

    and compares it with the Nootka translation:

    (B) *Tl'imshya'isita'itlma*

    Whorf comments as follows: 'Nootka has no parts of speech; the simplest utterance is a sentence, treating of some event or event-complex. Long sentences are sentences of sentences (complex sentences) not sentences of words. In (B) we have a simple not a complex Nootka sentence. The translation "he invites people to a feast" splits into subject and predicate. Not so the native sentence. It begins with the event of "boiling or cooking", *tl'imsh*; then comes *-ya* ("result") "cooked"; then *-'is* "eating" = "eating cooked food"; then *-ita* ("those who do") = "eaters of cooked food"; then *-'itl* ("going for") then *-ma*, sign of third person indicative, giving *tl'imshya'isita'itlma,* which answers to the crude paraphrase, "he, or somebody, goes for (invites) eaters of cooked food".'

Whorf adds, by way of explanation two (very different) pictorial models of the two sentences and says: 'Here are shown the different ways in which English and Nootka formulate the same event. The English sentence is divisible into subject and predicate; the Nootka sentence is not, yet it is complete and logical. Furthermore, the Nootka sentence is just one word, consisting of the root *tl'imsh* with five suffixes.'

This is by no means the only example Whorf gives and similar instances can be multiplied indefinitely from the literature. In particular, chapter iv of Sapir's classic *Language* provides some easily accessible examples. There is a convenient summary in chapter 1 of *Language, Thought and Culture,* Ed. Paul Henle (Ann Arbor, 1958).

31. For the limitations of translation, see for example, Quine (1960).
32. See O'Connor (1968), page 13.
33. See e.g. Sheehan (1972).
34. Tarski (1956), pages 152–278.
35. Tarski (1944), reprinted in Feigl and Sellars (1949).
36. ibid.
37. ibid.
38. ibid.
39. ibid.
40. ibid., page 61.
41. Tarski (1956), page 186.
42. op. cit., page 187.
43. op. cit., page 190.
44. op. cit., page 191.
45. op. cit., page 191.
46. op. cit., page 195.
47. op. cit., page 165.
48. In Feigl and Sellars (1949), page 65.
49. See e.g. Popper (1972), section 7; Montague (1970); Davidson (1970).
50. Mackie (1973).
51. In Feigl and Sellars (1949), page 70.
52. In Hanfling (1972), page 262.
53. Tarski (1956), page 62.
54. In Hanfling (1972), pages 274–5.
55. Tarski (1956), page 190.
56. Quine (1970), page 36.
57. Tarski (1956), page 191.
58. Tarski (1956), page 194.
59. Quine (1970), page 38.
60. ibid.
61. Reprinted in Pitcher (1964), pages 18–53.
62. op. cit., page 21.
63. op. cit., page 22.
64. op. cit., page 20.

65. op. cit., page 22.
66. op. cit., page 24.
67. ibid.
68. ibid.
69. op. cit., page 25.
70. op. cit., page 22.
71. op. cit., page 51.
72. op. cit., page 32.
73. In Pitcher (1964).
74. Pitcher (1964), page 36.
75. op. cit., page 37.
76. op. cit., page 37.
77. op. cit., page 39.
78. op. cit., page 36–7.
79. op. cit., page 38.
80. op. cit., page 37.
81. op. cit., page 39.
82. Davidson (1967).
83. Pitcher (1964), page 39.
84. Strawson (1971), pages 234–50.
85. op. cit., page 239.
86. Pitcher (1964), page 53.
87. Strawson (1949).
88. In Pitcher (1964), pages 16–17.
89. White (1970), page 92.
90. Strawson (1949), page 84.
91. op. cit., page 93.
92. Strawson (1949), page 84.
93. 'A Problem about Truth' reprinted in Strawson (1971).
94. Stegmüller (1957), page 229.
95. Pitcher (1964), pages 42–3.
96. op. cit., page 32.
97. *Republic*, Book vii.
98. Wittgenstein (1973), page 21.
99. See, e.g. Searle (1965).
100. Goodman (1969), page 3.

Bibliography

ACTON, H. B. (1935). 'The Correspondence Theory of Truth', *Proceedings of the Aristotelian Society*, **35**.

AUSTIN, J. L. (1950). 'Truth', *Proceedings of the Aristotelian Society*, suppl. vol. **24**. Reprinted in *Truth* (Ed. G. Pitcher).

AYER, A. J. (1963). 'Truth' in *The Concept of a Person*. London.

BLACK, M. (1948). 'The Semantic Definition of Truth', *Analysis*, **8**.

BLANSHARD, B. (1939). *The Nature of Thought*. 2 vols. London.

CARNAP, R. (1951). *Meaning and Necessity*. 2nd ed. Chicago.

CARTWRIGHT, R. L. (1962). 'Propositions', *Analytical Philosophy*, Ed. R. J. Butler. Oxford.

CHISHOLM, R. M. (1966). *The Theory of Knowledge*. Englewood Cliffs.

CHOMSKY, N. (1972). *Language and Mind*. 2nd ed. New York.

COHEN, L. J. (1964). 'Do Illocutionary Forces Exist?', *Philosophical Quarterly*, **14**, no. 55.

COUSIN, D. R. (1950). 'Truth', *Proceedings of the Aristotelian Society,* suppl. vol. **24**.

DAITZ, E. (1953). 'The Picture Theory of Meaning', *Mind*, **62**, no. 246.

DAVIDSON, D. (1967). 'Truth and Meaning', *Synthese*, **17**, no. 3.

DAVIDSON, D. (1970). 'Semantics for Natural Languages' in *Linguaggio nella Società e nella Technica*. Milan.

DUMMETT, M. (1958–9). 'Truth', *Proceedings of the Aristotelian Society*, **59**. Reprinted in Pitcher (1964).

EATON, R. M. (1925). *Symbolism and Truth*. Cambridge, Mass.

EWING, A. C. (1934). *Idealism: A Critical Survey*. London.

FEIGL, H. and SELLARS, W. (1949). *Readings in Philosophical Analysis*. New York.

FODOR, J. A. and KATZ, J. J. (1964). *The Structure of Language*. Englewood Cliffs.

GEACH, P. T. (1956). *Mental Acts*. London.

GEACH, P. T. (1965). 'Assertion', *Philosophical Review*, **14**, no. 4.

GOODMAN, N. (1969). *Languages of Art*. Oxford.

HAMLYN, D. W. (1962). 'The Correspondence Theory of Truth', *Philosophical Quarterly*, **12**.

HAMLYN, D. W. (1971). *The Theory of Knowledge*. London and New York.

HANFLING, O. (Ed.) (1972). *Fundamental Problems in Philosophy*. Oxford.

HERBST, P. (1952). 'The Nature of Facts', *Australasian Journal of Philosophy*, **30**.

HOCKETT, C. F. (1958). *A Course in Modern Linguistics*. New York.

KLUCKHOHN, C. and LEIGHTON, D. (1946). *The Navaho*. Cambridge, Mass.

KÖRNER, S. (1955). 'Truth as a Predicate', *Analysis*, **15**.

KÖRNER, S. (1955). *Conceptual Thinking*. Cambridge.

LEMMON, E. J. (1966). 'Sentences, Statements and Propositions', *British Analytical Philosophy*, Ed. B. Williams and A. Montefiore. London.

LEONARD, H. (1967). *Principles of Reasoning*. New York.

LUCAS, J. R. (1958). 'On Not Worshipping Facts', *Philosophical Quarterly*, **8.**

MACKIE, J. L. (1952). 'The Nature of Facts', *Australasian Journal of Philosophy*, **30.**

MACKIE, J. L. (1973). *Truth, Probability and Paradox*. Oxford.

MCKINSEY, J. C. (1948–9). 'A New Theory of Truth', *Synthese*, **7.**

MCTAGGART, J. M. E. (1921 and 1927). *The Nature of Existence*. 2 vols. Cambridge.

MONTAGUE, R. (1970). 'English as a Formal Language' in *Linguaggio nella Società e nella Tecnica*. Milan.

O'CONNOR, D. J. (1968). 'Beliefs, Dispositions & Actions', *Proceedings of the Aristotelian Society*.

PENN, Julia M. (1972). *Linguistic Relativity versus Innate Ideas*. The Hague.

PITCHER, G. (Ed.) (1964). *Truth*. Englewood Cliffs.

POPPER, K. R. (1972). *Objective Knowledge*. Oxford.

PRICE, H. H. (1934). 'Some Considerations about Belief', *Proceedings of the Aristotelian Society*, **35.**

PRICE, H. H. (1953). *Thinking and Experience*. London.

PRICE, H. H. (1969). *Belief*. London.

PRIOR, A. N. (1967). 'The Correspondence Theory of Truth' in *Encyclopedia of Philosophy*, Ed. Paul Edwards. New York.

QUINE, W. V. O. (1960). *Word and Object*. Cambridge, Mass.

QUINE, W. V. O. (1969). 'Propositional Objects' in *Ontological Relativity and Other Essays*. New York.

QUINE, W. V. O. (1970). *Philosophy of Logic*. Englewood Cliffs.

RAMSEY, F. P. (1927). 'Facts and Propositions', *Proceedings of the Aristotelian Society*, suppl. vol. **7.** Reprinted (in part) in Pitcher (1964).

RUSSELL, B. (1912). *The Problems of Philosophy*. London.

RUSSELL, B. (1914). *Our Knowledge of the External World*. London.

RUSSELL, B. (1949). *An Inquiry into Meaning and Truth*. New York and London.

RUSSELL, B. (1956). 'Facts and Propositions' in *The Philosophy of Logical Atomism*, reprinted in *Logic and Knowledge*, Ed. R. C. Marsh. London.

RYLE, G. (1930). 'Are there Propositions', *Proceedings of the Aristotelian Society*, **30.**

SAPIR, E. (1921). *Language*. New York.

SAPIR, E. (1931). 'Conceptual Categories of Primitive Languages', *Science*, **74**, 578.

SEARLE, J. R. (1965). 'What is a Speech Act?', *Philosophy in America*, Ed. Max Black. London.

SELLARS, W. (1959). 'Truth and Correspondence', *Journal of Philosophy*, **56.**

VON SENDEN, M. (1960). *Space and Sight*. London. Trans. P. L. Heath. London.

SHEEHAN, P. W. (Ed.) (1972). *The Function & Nature of Imagery*. New York and London.

STEGMÜLLER, W. (1957). *Das Wahrheitsproblem und die Idee der Semantik*. Vienna.

STRAWSON, P. F. (1949). 'Truth', *Analysis*, **9,** no. 6.

STRAWSON, P. F. (1950). 'Truth', *Proceedings of the Aristotelian Society*, suppl. vol. **24.** Reprinted in *Truth* (Ed. G. Pitcher) and in *Logico-Linguistic Papers* (London, 1971).

STRAWSON, P. F. (1971). *Logico-Linguistic Papers*. London.

TARSKI, A. (1944). 'The Semantic Conception of Truth', *Philosophy and Phenomenological Research*, **4.** Reprinted in Feigl & Sellars (1949).

TARSKI, A. (1956). 'The Concept of Truth in Formalised Languages' in *Logic, Semantics and Metamathematics*. Trans. J. Woodger. Oxford.

TARSKI, A. (1969). 'Truth and Proof', *Scientific American*, June. Reprinted in *Fundamental Problems of Philosophy*, Ed. O. Hanfling. Oxford.

VENDLER, Z. (1967). 'Facts and Events' in *Linguistics in Philosophy*. Ithaca.

WARNOCK, G. J. 'A Problem about Truth' in Pitcher (1969).

WHITE, A. R. (1970). *Truth*. London and New York.

WHORF, B. L. (1956). *Language, Thought and Reality*. Ed. J. B. Carrol. Cambridge, Mass.

WILLIAMS, C. F. J. (1969). 'What does "X is true" say about X?', *Analysis*, **29.**

WITTGENSTEIN, L. (1922). *Tractatus Logico-Philosophicus*. Trans. C. K. Ogden. London.

WITTGENSTEIN, L. (1973). *Letters to C. K. Ogden*. Ed. G. H. von Wright. Oxford and London.

WOOZLEY, A. D. (1949). *Theory of Knowledge*. London.

Index